It's another Quality Book from CGP

This book is for 11-14 year olds.

Whatever subject you're doing it's the same
old story — there are lots of facts and you've just got
to learn them. KS3 English is no different.

The good news, however, is that this CGP book delivers
the hard cold facts as clearly as possible.

It's also got some daft bits in to try and make the whole
experience at least vaguely entertaining for you.

What CGP is all about

Our sole aim here at CGP is to produce the highest quality
books — carefully written, immaculately presented and
dangerously close to being funny.

Then we work our socks off to get them out to you
— at the cheapest possible prices.

Contents

READING COMPREHENSION

QUOTING

SHAKESPEARE

WRITING

SECTION SIX — WRITING QUESTIONS

SECTION SEVEN — PARAGRAPHS

SECTION EIGHT — WRITING PROPERLY

SECTION NINE — MAKING IT INTERESTING

SECTION TEN — PERSUASIVE WRITING

Published by Coordination Group Publications Ltd.

Contributors:
Angela Billington
Taissa Csáky
Dominic Hall
Gemma Hallam
Sharon Keeley
Simon Little
Katherine Reed
Laura Schibrowski
Katherine Stewart
Tim Wakeling
James Paul Wallis
Andrew Wright

ISBN: 978 1 84762 157 3

Groovy website: www.cgpbooks.co.uk
Jolly bits of clipart from CorelDRAW®
Printed by Elanders Hindson Ltd, Newcastle upon Tyne.

Reading Questions

Reading questions ask you to write about bits of writing you haven't seen before.
They make up a whole paper in your English SATs — so you'd best know how to do them.

Reading Questions Aren't as Difficult as you Think

You get a few bits of writing to read, and some questions about each one.
Don't try to make a big deal about it — you can get good marks by making very simple points.

Three Golden Rules

1) Make simple points in your answers.

2) Get all your answers from the text — don't make things up.

3) Quote to back up your answer whenever you can.

Read Each Piece of Writing Carefully

Yes, this is a dead obvious piece of advice.
It's worth saying though — you don't want to lose a load of marks for
something so silly as not reading the questions or the bits of writing properly.

(1) Read each bit of writing carefully, so you
know what it's about and what happens.

(2) Then read through all the questions.

(3) After you've read the questions, read through the first bit of writing
again with the questions in your mind. Once you know what the
questions are, you might spot some things you hadn't seen before.

Oops!

Straightforward?...

It Really IS that Straightforward...

All you have to do after that is answer each question in turn.
The next few pages tell you how to do just that...

Life under The Pharaohs — the golden rule...

The worst thing that can happen in an exam is when you think you can't answer the questions.
But learn those three golden rules and you'll be ready for anything they throw at you.
Make sure you use them for every reading question and you'll be fine. There — couldn't be better?

State the Obvious

This is a <u>really important</u> piece of advice. Don't be scared — you don't have to get all complicated to do well in English SATs. You get <u>plenty</u> of marks for stating the <u>obvious</u>.

You get marks if you State The <u>Obvious</u>

I don't blame you if you read the questions and think "I can't think of <u>anything</u> clever to say." Don't worry — think of something <u>obvious</u> to say. Sensible points that you make will get you marks, even if they hardly seem worth saying at first.

If you notice something in the <u>text</u> that seems to answer the <u>question</u>, the chances are it <u>does</u> answer the question, so <u>write it down</u>.

<u>DON'T</u> think "Oh, that's obvious, there's no point in putting that". Of <u>course</u> there's a point — the point is you'll <u>get marks</u> for writing it down.

Here's an Example of Making <u>Simple Points</u>

Look at this example...

Here's a question:

Q. What does the writer tell us about Lee's feelings in the dentist's waiting room?

Here's a bit of a story:

> Lee shivered. He pulled his coat tightly around him, although it wasn't cold. His fists were clenched in his pockets. He stared at the floor in front of his feet and occasionally glanced nervously at the other people in the waiting room.

Here goes — the <u>answer</u>.

Here's a bit from the text that's got something to do with the question.

I'm staring at the floor too!

The writer tells us that Lee was nervous and scared. Lee "glanced nervously" at the other people in the waiting room. The writer says he was shivering, "although it wasn't cold". He was staring at the floor, which people often do when they're nervous.

Shivering and scared go together, so mention that he was shivering.

This answer may sound <u>simple</u>, but it's <u>all you need</u> to do to get the marks.

I'm in a bit of a state — California, I think...

This is the <u>ultra-important</u> bit of advice for tackling reading questions. <u>Learn</u> it before you go any further. Even <u>dead obvious</u> things are worth saying — they get you more marks.

Two Great Tips for Reading

There are some things <u>no one</u> likes to admit. 1) Pretending the examiners are <u>thick</u> is a great tip.
2) Writing <u>properly</u> gets you more marks.

Pretend <u>the</u> Examiners <u>are</u> Thick

This sounds bizarre, but it's actually a <u>really good tip</u>.

Imagine that you have to <u>explain everything</u> to them because they don't understand anything.

This goes back to the point about stating the obvious. If you don't make the really <u>simple</u> points, the examiner might <u>not know</u> that you <u>have</u> thought about them.

There's nothing worse than making a fabulously clever point and losing out on marks because the examiner <u>doesn't</u> quite <u>understand</u> what you're getting at.

Make sure what you write is easy to <u>understand</u>.

I wouldn't try anything like this if I were you...

The writer has made Lee a metaphor for the primeval fear which resides in all human kind. The writer identifies his fears with the physical sensation of shivering, giving him a universal, almost Christ-like humanity and calling on our deepest wellsprings of sympathy and self-awareness.

It Doesn't Hurt <u>to Write</u> Properly

You don't get any marks for handwriting. But if the Examiner's just looked at <u>300</u> disgustingly <u>untidy answers</u> and yours is the <u>first nice neat one</u> that hits their eyes, they're going to like you. You bet they are.

Writing in <u>proper sentences</u> with proper <u>punctuation</u> will make it easier for the examiner to understand the points you're making. Make sure you use the right punctuation for <u>quoting</u> — see <u>Section 3</u> for how to do it properly.

Split your answer into <u>paragraphs</u>, one for each of your main points. It'll make it crystal clear to the examiners that you've made lots of <u>separate points</u> and you deserve <u>lots of marks</u>.

Thick examiners — about eight inches across...

Horrible messy writing not proper sentence understand hard very. And remember to pretend that the examiner doesn't know what you're writing about. Explain things properly and make their day.

Short Reading Questions

Most of the questions on the Reading paper are itsy-bitsy <u>short</u> ones.
No yellow-polka-dot-bikinis though.

The <u>Short Questions</u> Don't Look Too Bad

1) Some of the short questions are really <u>easy</u>.
2) But some of them need you to do a bit of <u>thinking</u>.
3) Read <u>each question</u> a couple of times before you try answering it so you don't muck up.

Some Questions Check You Understand

These questions are testing that you <u>understand</u> what you've read.
They're not that hard, so don't make a <u>big deal</u> out of them.

Lick your lips if you understand

> From paragraph 3, write down how long the Headless Horseman has been living at the inn.

They could ask you to <u>find bits</u> from the writing and <u>write them down</u>.

> From the fifth paragraph, give three ways in which goblins are different from trolls.

They could ask you to <u>sum up</u> part of the writing.

Most Short Questions Ask You About the Style

Most of the short questions ask about <u>the way things are written</u>.

> Explain how the first paragraph sets a **gloomy** tone.

The trick with style questions is to look at the <u>detail</u>.
Look at <u>each word</u> and decide what it's doing there.

Mention any gloomy <u>words</u> in your answer.

> The hooded man reined in his horse, and wiped the blood from his face. He strained his eyes and ears for a sign that he was nearing safety, but the black night suffocated all sight and sound.

Darn shaving cuts

Write about what's <u>happening</u> too. It tells you the man's in trouble and that <u>adds</u> to the gloominess.

<u>Everything</u> you need to answer reading questions is there <u>in the texts</u>.
<u>Keep reading</u> until you <u>find</u> the answer. <u>Don't</u> make things up.

Clogs or wellies — it's all a question of style...

The trick with these short questions is not to get <u>cocky</u>. If you assume they're <u>all</u> easy you could make some nasty mistakes. Read each one through a couple of times and you'll be fine.

Working Out What to Do

Here's what you need to look at on every question to be sure you're doing what they want.

They Tell You Where to Find the Answer

The question always tells you where to look for the answer.

> Explain how the final paragraph is an effective ending for the story.

> From paragraph four, write down two reasons why goblins should not be fed soup.

Don't waste time going through the whole piece of writing for each question. Just go straight to the paragraph they tell you to look at.

If the question says "From paragraph 4..." then look at paragraph 4. The answer will be in there somewhere.

Give them What they Ask For

Some questions make life really easy because they tell you what to write.

 write down **two phrases**...

For this you just need to copy two phrases from the piece you've read.

When they say this, be sure to get that quote in your answer — if you forget it you'll lose a mark.

 Support your answer with a **quotation**...

write down **three reasons**...

Be darn sure you give three reasons — not two or four.

Open-ended Questions Are Trickier

Some questions don't tell you exactly what to say — you have to work it out.

How does the author *blah*...

Explain **how** the author *blahs*...

If the question asks how, use by in your answer.

The author creates a spooky atmosphere by...

Explain **why** *blah*...

If the question asks why, use because in your answer.

The author writes in short sentences because...

For more on this type of question, see P. 20.

Examiners are crazy — paragraph-obsessive...

In nine situations out of ten, the best thing to do is have a slice of cake. If your school doesn't allow cake in the exam hall, you'll have to do the second best thing and get on with the test.

How Much to Write

This page is all about making sure you do <u>just the right amount</u> to get the marks.
Write <u>too much</u> and you're wasting time. Write <u>too little</u>, and you definitely won't get full marks.

Look at the Number of Marks

At the bottom of each question it tells you <u>how many marks</u> you can get for it.
Short questions are worth...

1 mark   2 marks <u>or</u> 3 marks

1) For a <u>1 mark</u> question you only need to make one point, find one phrase or give one word.
2) If the question's worth <u>2 marks</u> you'll need to have two bits to your answer.
3) For <u>3 mark</u> questions you'll need to make three points —
   you won't get three marks for a one-word answer.

The Answer Space Shows You How Much to Write

The <u>space</u> for writing the answer gives you a <u>massive clue</u> to how much you should write.

When they give you <u>bullet points</u>, put one point for each.

• <u>implosion</u>

If there's just a small space write in <u>notes</u>, or give a <u>one-word answer</u>.

• Feeding soup to goblins can make them implode.
• Giving soup to goblins reminds them of the war.

If the lines go all the way across the page write a <u>sentence</u>.

...and one for papa...

For <u>grids</u> it's OK to write in note form. Write something in <u>all</u> the empty boxes.

	Goblins	Trolls
Author's attitude	*thinks they're disgusting*	*admires trolls*
Phrase showing author's attitude	*"fetid stench"*	*"superhuman strength"*

If you can't fit your answer into the space you've written <u>too much</u>.
Read through the question again and check <u>exactly</u> what they wanted.

If your answer <u>hardly</u> fills the space at all something's gone a bit wrong.
You've probably <u>missed something</u> in the piece you had to read. Have <u>another look</u> at it.

Answer space — the final frontier...

This page is easier than falling off a <u>greasy log</u>. Just two simple things you need to remember —
write enough to get the marks, and use <u>all</u> the space they give you for writing your answers.

Mini-Essay Questions

The last question for some texts is a bit <u>longer</u>. You have to do a little <u>mini-essay</u>. Fun, fun, fun.

The <u>Mini-Essay Questions</u> Look Like This

Dashed question must be round here somewhere.

These questions ask about <u>the whole text</u> — don't get stuck in the first couple of paragraphs. Make sure you write about the whole thing.

In the whole text, how does the author mix horror and humour?

You should comment on:
— how the author describes the Goblins
— how the author describes the Trolls
— whether you think there is more horror or humour in the story

(5 marks)

If they give you <u>hints</u>, use them to organise your answer. Write about each one in turn.

You won't <u>always</u> get hints. If you don't, you should still aim to have at least <u>three main chunks</u> to your answer.

You get <u>5 marks</u> for these longer questions. Make one or two points for <u>each</u> of the hints. <u>Back up</u> each point with a <u>quote</u> for full marks.

Don't Spend Ages <u>on the Long Questions</u>

These mini-essays will take a bit <u>longer</u> to do than the shorter questions. Obviously. But you <u>don't</u> have time to muck about.

1) Go back to the piece you've read. Pick out the bits you're going to write about — <u>underline</u> the bits that answer the question, or put <u>stars</u> in the margin.

2) Once you start writing don't do anything fancy. Stick to <u>clear simple English</u>. <u>Make a point</u>, back it up with a <u>quote</u>, and move on to your next point. Keep going till you've made <u>at least</u> 5 decent points.

3) Have a quick read through what you've written to make sure you haven't said anything <u>blatantly stupid</u>.

4) Go on to the <u>next question</u>.

It's over here, dozy butt.

The main thing is not to get <u>bogged down</u>. If you really <u>dry up</u> on one of these questions, leave it. Do all the short questions first, then <u>come back</u> at the end.

Mini-essay — I'd rather have a mini-egg...

These questions are a bit harder than the short questions. But not <u>that</u> much harder. Don't be intimidated by them. Stand up to them. Show the <u>little blighters</u> what you're made of, what-ho.

What Questions Mean

If you want to <u>write a good answer</u>, you'd better make sure that you <u>understand the question</u>.

Work Out What The Question Wants You To Do

Sometimes, the questions aren't quite as straightforward as they might be.
But those hard-looking questions actually just want you to do a few not-so-hard things.

Look at these questions — and <u>see what they really want you to do</u>.

> **Q. How is suspense created in this story?**
>
> ① Write about <u>the things</u> that happen in the story.
>
> ② Write about <u>the words</u> that the writer uses.
>
> ③ Write about <u>the way the story is put together</u> — does the writer leave some things out to make you wonder what's going on?

I feel suspended...

Break it down into easy bits before you try to answer it.

Write about <u>the words the writer chooses</u> to make the castle seem interesting.

Q. In what <u>way</u> does the article make you want to visit the castle?

Say what the writer <u>tells readers about the castle</u>.

Write about <u>the way the writer ends the article</u> — does the writer decide that the castle is worth visiting?

Look out for Key Words in the Question

Work out what <u>kind</u> of question it is. These <u>key words</u> are a massive clue.

Q. <u>How</u> does the <u>writer</u>...

You <u>always</u> have to talk about the <u>words</u> the writer uses and the way the piece is <u>put together</u> for this kind of question.

Who needs key words when you've got a key nose...

Q. How does the writer <u>build up a picture</u> of...

Talk about the <u>words</u> the writer uses. If it's a <u>story</u>, talk about the <u>reactions</u> of the <u>narrator</u> and the characters.

Q. What is your <u>impression</u> of the shopkeeper?

Write about <u>what kind</u> of person the shopkeeper is. Say which bits you've used to get your answer.

Different Questions

Different questions need answering in different ways.
It's worth looking out for key words in the question to help you decide how to answer it.

Make Your Answer Fit The Question

1) Different questions can ask about the same thing in different ways.

2) Don't fall into the trap of thinking "This is a question about blurg, so I'll just write about blurg".

3) You really have to look for those key words, and be really sure what the question wants you to do.

Both these questions basically mean "write about the supervisor at the doorknob factory" — but you'll get precious extra marks if you tackle them in slightly different ways:

The key words in this question are "What impression". This is a simple, open question. It's asking you to comment on what the supervisor says and does.

Q. What impression do you get of the supervisor at the doorknob factory?

The key words here are "How does the writer". This is a bit more specific. You need to write about the writer's use of language.

Q. How does the writer make you dislike the supervisor at the doorknob factory?

You also get a handy hint with this question — the word "dislike". You know you're looking for things that show the supervisor in a bad light.

How To Make Your Answer Fit The Question

Here's what you might do differently to answer these two questions.
Both answers talk about the same thing, but from slightly different angles.

Q. What impression do you get of the supervisor at the doorknob factory?

Q. How does the writer make you dislike the supervisor at the doorknob factory?

The supervisor of the doorknob factory treats the workers badly. She thinks they are useless, and keeps threatening them with the sack.

The writer spends a long time describing how the supervisor treats her workers. The writer uses words like "yells", "threatened" and "a sarcastic laugh" to show how the supervisor speaks to the workers.

This answer talks about **WHAT** the writer says in the story.

This answer talks about **HOW** the writer says it.

This is about choice of words and structure.

Like a chef deciding **WHAT** to cook.

Like a chef deciding **HOW** to cook it.

Questions About Language

When they ask questions about the language, you have to write about the <u>words</u> that a writer chooses to <u>describe</u> things. This page shows you what to do, so <u>learn</u> it.

Write about Descriptions

If you're asked <u>how</u> a writer creates a <u>picture</u> of something, you'll have to write about the <u>words</u> that he or she uses to describe it.

The rustling noise grew louder and more persistent. When it started, Marcie had thought of leaves blowing in the wind, but now it was far too loud for that. It sounded like someone stomping through crisp packets. The rustling turned into crunching, as if some huge animal was munching on a gigantic cream cracker.

The bits in red give you an idea of a really loud crunching sound.

Does the Writer Finish the Description all in One Go?

Often, a writer <u>won't</u> describe the thing they're talking about all in one go. This often happens in stories when a <u>new character</u> or <u>place</u> is introduced to the readers — the writer tells you about them a bit at a time. If you notice this, write about it in your answer. It'll get you <u>more</u> marks.

Write about Words used to Create a Mood

Questions that ask things like "How does the writer <u>build up tension</u>?" look rather nasty. First of all, you need to <u>find words</u> that give you an <u>idea</u> of <u>tension</u> or <u>alarm</u>. Then see how the writer <u>increases</u> the fear and alarm felt by the <u>narrator</u> and the characters in the story.

Her words sure put him in a mood

You big, ugly monster!

Hmmf.

At first, the narrator is "slightly suspicious" of the man in the green jumper. The writer builds up the narrator's feeling of alarm as she realises that the man is up to no good. She becomes "more and more afraid". The writer describes the narrator's fear when she thinks the man has seen her. This creates tension. The tension is kept up right until the man leaves the museum.

<u>Nothing</u> in the writing is the way it is by <u>accident</u>. The writer has <u>chosen</u> words <u>deliberately</u> to make the readers feel happy, or sad, or tense, or excited or whatever.

Structure

If you're asked about <u>how the writer does something</u> in the story it's always worth writing about how the piece is actually <u>put together</u>. It won't have been written that way by accident.

Are the <u>Beginning</u> and <u>End Different</u>?

You can get <u>asked</u> about this in the Exam, so pay attention.
Sometimes the very <u>end</u> of a piece is written in a slightly <u>different style</u> to create an effect.

Beginning   End

For example, when a writer is trying to <u>persuade</u> readers, he or she might round the piece off by talking in a direct and friendly way about his or her <u>own experience</u>.

<u>Non-fiction</u> articles that <u>start</u> with a question of some sort will <u>end</u> by answering the question. This rounds the article off nicely.

Well, I *think* it's different...

In conclusion, we can answer the question posed at the beginning of this article by saying that criminals should be rehabilitated as well as punished.

Does the Writer seem to <u>Change</u> <u>his or her</u> <u>Opinion</u>?

Underwater Snooker by Ted Hanson
In the last few years, many bizarre new sports like pogo-stick racing and tree surfing have taken off.
One that seems unlikely to ever become popular is underwater snooker. I must admit, I laughed out loud when the idea was first suggested to me. I couldn't imagine why anyone would want to put on a wetsuit and climb into a swimming pool for a game of snooker.

I was invited to Sharky's Pool and Snooker Pool, and after a couple of games I was hooked. The experience of potting a ball six feet underwater is something that has to be tried.

It's rubbish!
It's brilliant!
The writer has changed his mind. He's decided he likes underwater snooker.

It <u>isn't</u> that the writer <u>can't</u> make his mind up. He's actually changing his opinion <u>on purpose</u>. He starts off by saying that underwater snooker is crazy — that's something that most readers would <u>agree</u> with. Then he says that <u>he's</u> been <u>convinced</u> by a visit to a snooker pool. He wants readers to <u>agree</u> with him here, too.

Termites love structures — especially wooden ones...

The way that the piece is <u>put together</u> is as important as the <u>words</u> the writer uses for those "how does the writer?" type of questions. Remember — the writer did it that way <u>on purpose</u>.

Questions Asking for Your Opinion

Some questions ask you specifically for <u>what you think</u>.
This is another kind of question that you need to tackle in a <u>slightly different</u> way.

Watch Out For Questions That Want Your Opinion

It's normally a <u>bad idea</u> to write "<u>I think</u>" or "<u>in my opinion</u>" in your reading question answers.
The only time you should is if the question specifically asks what you think.

These two questions are very <u>similar</u>, but you'll get more marks for tackling them <u>differently</u>.

The key words are "do you think".

> **In what ways does the article try to persuade people to watch more movies?**

Write about what the article says <u>and</u> how it says it.

> **Do you think the article will persuade people to watch more movies?**

With this question you need to write about what the article says and how it says it, <u>AND</u> say <u>how effective</u> you think it is.

This is the way to watch more movies.

How To Answer Opinion Questions

There's no big <u>secret</u> about answering questions that ask what you think. You just have to remember to <u>give reasons</u> for what you think. These can be pretty much the same things you would write to answer a normal question.

> **In what ways does the article try to persuade people to watch more movies?**

> **Do you think the article will persuade people to watch more movies?**

The article says that watching movies is a good way to escape from real life for a couple of hours.

You won't escape next time Mr. Pond.

REAL LIFE

I think it will persuade people because everyone needs to forget their troubles for a couple of hours every now and then.

This answer talks about a <u>point</u> the article makes.

This says that <u>you think</u> it's a good point — and it says <u>WHY</u> you think so.

Exams are rubbish — that's my opinion...

Opinion questions are great — you get to say what you think. Just make sure you give <u>reasons</u>, or you'll be throwing marks away. <u>Don't</u> give your opinion unless the question asks you to.

Finding the Important Bits

The hard thing is finding the bit of the writing that tells you the answer to the question.

Find the bits that Answer the Question

> **Q. In what way does the article make readers want to visit the Castle?**

The key to answering questions like this is to find loads of things in the article that help answer the question. Here's the start of the article with the bits you need and the bits you don't need helpfully pointed out...

Callendale Castle, often called one of the finest castles in England, is built on a hill overlooking the village of Callendale in West Bassetshire. On approaching Callendale village, the twin towers of the castle suddenly loomed through the mist, giving the village a mysterious appearance.

Callendale Castle holds many stories, and many secrets. A quick read through the guidebook gave me a colourful insight into the way things must have been inside these forbidding stone walls all those years ago. A secret meeting between King Henry V and a French ambassador took place here during the Hundred Years War. In 1814, the castle narrowly escaped being burnt to the ground when a lazy kitchen boy left a pig roasting on the open fire unattended.

The castle tour took me to a dark, dank dungeon, complete with gruesome instruments of torture. Hidden in one corner is a tiny cell, little more than a hole, where countless prisoners were left to rot away. It is hard to imagine how a grown person could fit into a space so small.

Next, the Armoury Museum conjured up the blood and excitement of a medieval battle. During my visit, a party of schoolchildren were gleefully discussing which of the various gleaming swords they would prefer to have their heads chopped off with — which put me right off my lunch.

You DON'T need to say where the castle is.

Mention that it looks mysterious — that makes it sound interesting.

People would want to visit to find out more about the stories and secrets.

You DON'T need to retell these stories in your answer. Just say that the writer mentions them.

The writer spends some time talking about the dungeon. People find horrible things fascinating, so this bit is important.

This bit shows the schoolchildren enjoyed visiting the castle.

There'll be a Lot of things that Aren't Important

There'll always be a great load of stuff that's got nothing to do with the question. Don't write about every tiny little thing — only write about the bits that the question asks for.

Panning for gold — pick out the good bits...

Nobody can teach you to pick out the important bits. You have to make sure you go through the text and get all the important bits out. Remember — not all of it will be important.

Question Pointers

This is a <u>massively important</u> page.   Face it, losing a whole grade because you didn't <u>read the question properly</u> would be pretty embarrassing.   Don't let it happen — <u>learn</u> this page.

Always Use The Question Pointers

Often a question will be followed by some <u>pointers</u> telling you <u>what to put</u> in your <u>answer</u>. Whatever you do, don't ignore these pointers.   They're much more than helpful hints from the examiners — they're your ticket to <u>better marks</u>.   You'd have to be <u>mad</u> to ignore them.

> **How does the writer try to make you feel sympathy for Mr Hobscuttle?**
> In your answer you should comment on:
> • the way his childhood is described;
> • the way the supervisor at the doorknob factory treats him;
> • the way his relationship with his wife changes.

Write about <u>all</u> of these things.

When it says "you should" it <u>means</u> "you must", and no excuses.

If you write two half-decent paragraphs about <u>each</u> of these three points, you'll get <u>better</u> marks than if you write a brilliant long answer that <u>only</u> talks about <u>one</u> of them.

Write About All of the Points

① Don't miss <u>any</u> of the points out.   Write about <u>all</u> of them.   If you forget to write about one of the points, you will <u>lose marks</u>, and that's <u>guaranteed</u>. Your mark could actually go down a <u>whole level</u> — a <u>seriously hefty</u> drop.

Hey! You forgot to write about me!

• the way his relationship with his wife changes.

Oops.

I felt something drop!

② Try to spend a roughly <u>equal</u> amount of <u>time</u> talking about each of the pointers they give you. It doesn't have to be exact, but it shouldn't be far off.

Don't go off the rails — use all the points...

You either learn this or you've had it, basically.   When the question says "You should <u>comment</u> on..." it really means "You <u>must</u> write about...".   Every year, people lose out on <u>easy marks</u> because they don't <u>follow</u> what the question says.   Don't be one of them...

Writing your Answer

You need to know how to <u>put your answer together</u>. Once again, it's all about getting the <u>best possible</u> marks for your answer. So, it looks like you need to get this page <u>learned</u>.

Start by saying How you Answer the Question

It's a <u>good idea</u> to give a little <u>introduction</u> to your answer. All it needs to do is say what your basic answer to the question is. It helps the Examiner to see that you're setting off in the <u>right direction</u>, so it'll help <u>you</u> get <u>more marks</u>.

This is the <u>basic idea</u> of your answer.

The writer makes us feel sympathy for Mr Hobscuttle by describing his life as unhappy. The writer shows us that other people are to blame for Mr Hobscuttle's misfortune.

Go through All of the Points in Turn

The question pointers actually make it a lot <u>easier</u> to put your answer together. Write about <u>each</u> of the points in turn. It really is that simple.

Through what?

Write about one point...

Mr Hobscuttle "always tried in vain" to please his father, which tells us that his father was never happy with anything he did. His parents didn't show him love...

...and then go on to the next.

<u>Linking phrases</u> like this show where your answer is <u>going</u>.

Another person who treats Mr Hobscuttle badly is the supervisor at the doorknob factory. She...

Make it Obvious that you're Answering the Question

Don't be afraid to be <u>blatant</u> and repeat phrases <u>directly</u> from the <u>question</u>.

It <u>makes</u> the Examiner notice that you've read the question carefully and you're doing your best to <u>answer</u> it.

Of course, you can't just leave it at that — you have to go on and <u>write more</u> about each point.

Only take phrases, not huge chunks, or the Examiner will think you're just copying it from the question and don't know what you're talking about (see P.30).

Another area of Mr Hobscuttle's life where the writer tries to make us feel sympathy for him is the way his relationship with his wife changes. For example, the writer says...

This bit comes from the question.

Chasing the milkman? — I said points, not pints...

It's those good old <u>question pointers</u> again. The idea here is that you use them to <u>help you</u> write a good answer. They're like a ready-made plan. Write about them <u>in order</u>, and there you go, one well-structured answer. See, it's <u>not hard</u>, you just have to <u>remember</u> to do it.

Revision Summary Questions

Way-hey, we made it to the end of the section. There's quite a lot to get to grips with here, and you do need to know it all. There's nothing worse than losing marks because you didn't read the question properly. The best way to make sure you've got everything from this section stored away in that slimey sponge of a brain of yours is to go through the questions on this page over and over again until you're absolutely sure that you know the answers. If you don't, you can go back and check. Remember — the whole point of revision is to find out what you don't know, and then learn it until you do.

1) What are the three Golden Rules about Reading Questions?

2) Toad Girl reckons you shouldn't read the piece of writing first, but should skip straight to the questions. Is she right?

3) Is it okay to say simple, obvious things in your answers?

4) How does pretending the examiners are thick get you better marks?

5) Should you bother being neat?

6) Are questions that ask you what's going on:
   a) easypeasylemonsqueezy
   b) horrendous and not to be attempted
   c) straightforward so long as you read the question carefully?

7) For questions about style is it best to go into lots of detail or be nice and vague?

8) Do short questions tell you where to look for the answer?

9) If the question says "Write down 4 phrases..." should you write down:
   a) up to 4 phrases b) at least 4 phrases c) exactly 4 phrases?

10) Should you normally answer "how" questions with "by" or "because"?

11) Should you normally answer "why" questions with "by" or "because"?

12) If a question's worth 2 marks, how many bits are they expecting in your answer?

13) If you haven't got enough space to write your answer, what should you do?

14) Do the mini-essay questions ask about the odd paragraph, or the whole piece of writing?

15) Do you always get helpful hints on the mini-essay questions?

16) What would be different about your answers to these two questions?
   a) What impressions do you get of the giant mongoose?
   b) How does the writer make you like the giant mongoose?

17) When you get a question about how a piece of writing describes something or makes a picture of something, what do you need to look for so you can give an answer?

18) Is "check if the beginning and end are different"
   a) good advice, b) bad advice, or c) Elvis Presley's middle name?

19) What's the important thing to do for questions that ask you what <u>you think</u> about something?

20) Is it better to write about <u>all</u> the "in your answer you should comment on" points in a question, or to write a whole load about one or two of them?

21) How can you make it obvious that you're answering the question?

Only nine more sections to go...

Ooo, I can't wait...

Example — The Story

Read the story on this page and the next. Go on. It's not that bad.

In this extract, Jerry Derryberry has turned his unsuccessful bakery into a thriving business by selling skateboards for dogs.

Jerry Derryberry was sound asleep when the alarm clock chirped. He was awake in an instant, feeling bright and alert, not like in the old days when he had to struggle to rouse himself from a deep and dreamy slumber.

"Good morning, Kerry," he said cheerfully as he walked into the kitchen, where his wife was busy frying artichokes for breakfast. "Oh no," thought Jerry, "not artichokes again." He'd much rather just have a nice piece of toast. Jerry had been dropping hints for over a week now that he didn't like fried artichokes, but Kerry hadn't noticed. "I'd be quite happy with toast, you know, love."

"*Know Your Vegetables* magazine says the ancient Egyptians considered fried artichokes to be a source of health and strength," Kerry replied humourlessly, bringing two large plates of steaming artichokes to the table. Jerry groaned inwardly. In the past he might have got into an argument with Kerry about her silly magazines, but he was so happy at the success of his shop that he was much more able to cope with her these days.

"Those are bags under your eyes," Kerry said. "You should be sleeping more."

Jerry smiled patiently. "Don't be silly love," he said, "I sleep much more than you do."

Jerry was glad when breakfast was over and it was time to go to work. He positively bounced and skipped the ten minute walk to his shop, so full of energy was he feeling. The door to Jerry's bakery was open, and he could smell the sweet aroma of freshly baking bread. He filled his lungs and beamed with pride to think that this little shop, from which he had struggled to make a living for so long, was now beginning to build him an empire.

"Hello, Wayne," he called. "That smells wonderful. Will you be okay here in the shop while I check on the skateboard factory?"

"Sure thing, boss," Wayne responded. He was delighted to do anything the boss asked, since Jerry had given him that big pay rise.

Jerry closed the shop door behind him and went next door into the factory, which had been a dusty, long-deserted warehouse until he bought it and started manufacturing skateboards for dogs.

Example — The Story

As he closed the factory door behind him and surveyed the dozens of workers busily crafting pooch-sized skateboards, Jerry reflected on how long it had taken him to strike it lucky with one of his inventions. He used to sit at his desk until the early hours of the morning, tired after a long day at work, dreaming up ideas. He'd tried sleeping bags for fish, kangaroo binoculars, jigsaws for gerbils. None had caught on. But finally, he reflected, all those years of enterprise and hard work had paid off.

"What are you working on, Lisa?" he asked his chief designer.

"A new model for poodles," Lisa replied cheerfully. "We have to adapt our other designs because poodles have such small paws."

"Good, good," Jerry smiled benevolently. "Keep up the good work."

Jerry went back into the shop, where Wayne was serving a customer — a big-boned, jolly looking man who had a small, yapping white dog on a leash.

"I'm sorry, sir," Wayne was saying, "but none of our skateboards are suitable for poodles."

The man looked crestfallen. Smoothly, Jerry stepped in to assure him that a new model for poodles was being designed as he spoke. The customer's face brightened and the poodle, perhaps sensing his owner's mood, yapped happily. Jerry spent a moment thinking how wonderful it was that his idea had brought such pleasure into people's lives. Every day he saw customers' smiling faces in his shop, and it always gave him a warm glow of satisfaction.

"That's wonderful," the man said. "Oh, and I'll have a medium-sliced wholemeal loaf while I'm here, please."

Wayne extracted a freshly-baked wholemeal loaf from behind the counter and put it into the slicing machine. Meanwhile, an elderly lady walked in and looked in confusion at the display of dog skateboards lined up on the shelves. Jerry put a considerate arm around her and asked if she needed any help.

"I thought this was a bakery," she said. "I only wanted a nice sticky bun. I'm eighty-seven, you know." Jerry gave her a bun.

"There you are, my dear," he said. "You can have it for free."

From Derryberry's Dream Comes True, by I. O. Silver

... Who says you can't teach an old dog new tricks?

Shorter Questions

Right, you've read the story. The first questions you'll have to answer will be quite short. They put in questions like the ones on this page to test you understand the story.

Showing You Understand the Story

① The easiest questions of all ask you what's going on.

> From paragraph 6 on page 17 write down how long it took Jerry to walk to work.

Jerry was glad when breakfast was over and it was time to go to work. He positively bounced and skipped the ten minute walk to his shop...

There's the answer.
Stop reading and write it down.
It really is as simple as that.

② Some questions need a bit more work. You have to explain things from the story.

> From paragraph 1 on page 18, explain why Jerry is happier now than he was in the past.

The paragraph doesn't give the answer in an obvious way. You need to work it out. These are the bits that tell you the answer.

...dozens of workers busily crafting pooch-sized skateboards...

...used to sit at his desk until the early hours of the morning...

For your answer you could write:

> *In the past Jerry used to work hard without getting any results. Now he has dozens of people working for him, putting his ideas into practice.*

The answer doesn't have to be fancy or complicated to get the marks. It just has to be based on the story.

In Non-Fiction Writing You'll Have to Find Facts

You won't always get stories to read. They quite often put in articles from magazines, or leaflets and advertisements. For non-fiction they'll ask you to find facts, e.g.

> From paragraph 3, write down two benefits of seedless jam.

> From paragraph 7, write down one advantage and one disadvantage of selling jam in paper bags.

You answer these in exactly the same way — look at the paragraph, find as many examples as they're asking for, and write them down.

Reading test — name a large town on the Thames...

I'd like to ask the examiners a few questions. Like, why don't you leave us alone... What have we done to deserve this... What have we ever done to you... Do you think this is fair... Why...

Shorter Questions

Here are some <u>more</u> SAT-style questions. These ones are about the style —
they're testing whether you can see what fancy tricks the author's up to.

Go Into Detail on Style Questions

This question <u>sounds</u> vague and general — but that
doesn't mean you can give a <u>wishy-washy</u> answer.

> In the first paragraph, how does the
> writer show that Jerry enjoys life?

A good answer needs to go into <u>detail</u> about the story.
Read through the paragraph again, looking for <u>individual words</u> that tell you Jerry is happy.

> Jerry Derryberry was sound asleep when the alarm clock <u>chirped</u>. He was
> awake in an instant, feeling <u>bright and alert</u>, not like <u>in the old days</u> when
> he had to <u>struggle</u> to rouse himself from a deep and dreamy slumber.

Then explain how each word or phrase <u>adds</u> to the picture of Jerry as a man who enjoys life.

- *In the first sentence, the writer says the alarm clock "chirped".
  Alarm clocks usually make a horrible noise, and chirping is a
  pleasant sound, so this starts the story off on a positive note.*

  - *Jerry wakes up quickly, feeling "bright and alert".
    This suggests he looks forward to his day.*

*This looks like a lot of writing
about just a few words — but
you won't get any marks for just
putting a one-sentence answer.*

- *The writer draws a contrast in the second sentence between the present and the
  past. In "the old days" Jerry had to "struggle" to get out of bed. Now he wakes up
  quickly and happily. This contrast emphasises the idea that Jerry enjoys life now.*

Mistakes People Make on Style Questions

1. *The writer shows Jerry is happier now than he used to be.* ⬅ NO NO NO

   This <u>answer</u> is true enough but it doesn't answer the question.
   This person's written <u>about the plot</u> when they should have
   been writing about <u>the way the story's written</u>.

2. *The writer shows Jerry enjoys life by using happy words.* ⬅ BAD BAD BAD

   This answer is <u>sort of</u> true too. The trouble is it doesn't go
   into enough detail to get the marks. If it quoted some
   <u>actual words</u> from the story it would be WAY better.

Animal Farm was written in a pig-style...

Don't feel bad if you think this is <u>hard</u>. I think this is hard, and I'm a genius. Really, I am. Go
on, test me. I know my seven times tables and everything. And the <u>meaning of life</u>... *(crazed laughter)*

Mini-Essay Questions

The next four pages are about a <u>longer</u> question.

> **Q3. How does the writer describe Jerry's state of mind?**
>
> In your answer you should comment on:
> — the way Jerry reacts to his wife;
> — how he responds to his workplace;
> — the way he treats his employees;
> — how he reacts to his customers.

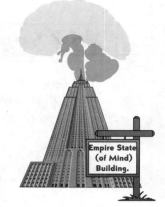

Empire State (of Mind) Building.

There's loads more that you could write for this one. Luckily, it gives you some <u>pointers</u> so you know which bits to concentrate on.

Before you even start to tackle this question, here are three bits of vitally <u>important</u> advice.

① <u>Write About All Of Those Pointers</u>

When it says "you should comment on," it <u>really</u> means "you <u>must</u> talk about".

Those pointers are worth their weight in gold. Read 'em and <u>use</u> 'em.

This question tells you to start off by talking about how Jerry behaves with his <u>wife</u>. Then talk about his <u>workplace</u>. Then his <u>employees</u> and then his <u>customers</u>. Try to write a roughly equal amount about each of them.

Do everything the pointers say and you're guaranteed to get <u>better marks</u>.

② <u>Think — Why Did The Writer Do It Like This</u>

Look at the <u>wording</u> of the question. This one starts "how does the writer <u>describe</u>...".

This story isn't just a <u>random</u> collection of thrown together words. It's been <u>deliberately</u> written by a writer who wants you to get something out of it.

When you answer the question, think about what the <u>writer</u> was <u>trying to do</u>.

For example, the writer didn't <u>need</u> to mention anything about Jerry's breakfast. The writer could've <u>skipped it</u> and started talking about Jerry at work. The breakfast scene is only there because the writer <u>thinks</u> it will <u>tell us something</u> about Jerry.

③ <u>Quote Like You've Never Quoted Before</u>

Quotes show the examiner you've got your answer <u>from the text</u>, not just made it up on a <u>whim</u>. More importantly <u>good quotes = good marks</u>. See <u>Section 3</u> for more on quoting.

Mini-Essay Questions

With those three bits of vital advice wanging round your head, let's <u>answer</u> the question.

If You <u>See</u> It, <u>Say</u> It — Start with Obvious Points

You have to start by talking about "the way Jerry reacts to his wife". <u>Read</u> that section of the story, and <u>write down points</u> as they occur to you. It doesn't matter if they're obvious.

I see SEA

> *The writer says that Jerry greets his wife "cheerfully". This shows he is in a happy state of mind.*

You might think this is so obvious it's hardly worth saying. Actually it's a great way to start your answer.

Starting with an <u>obvious</u> point often makes it easier to think of more <u>subtle</u> ones, like this.

Notice how it <u>links</u> closely to the story and uses two <u>quotes</u>. It also <u>explains</u> what this tells us about Jerry.

> *Jerry really doesn't want fried artichokes for breakfast — he'd "much rather" have toast. But despite that, he is very polite to his wife. All he says is that he'd be "quite happy" with toast. This shows how kind he is. He doesn't want to hurt her feelings.*

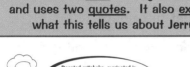

Roasted artichoke, marinated in cream and herb sauce and topped with finely toasted croutons, yum. It'll be ready in ten minutes.

Ummm, finely toasted...

Pay <u>Attention</u> To The Writer's <u>Choice</u> Of <u>Words</u>

This question asks you "<u>how does the writer describe...</u>". That makes it especially important to look at what <u>words</u> the writer has <u>chosen</u> to use. One single word can tell you a lot.

> *Jerry's wife annoys him but he doesn't let it show. He only groans "inwardly" rather than doing it out loud. That shows he's considerate.*

Here's a good example of how <u>one word</u> can tell you something important about a character.

I said choice of words, not choice of <u>woods</u>!

The writer <u>doesn't</u> use the word "patiently" by chance. He/she wants to show us that Jerry is generally a patient kind of guy.

> *The writer says that Jerry smiles "patiently". That shows that Jerry is patient with his wife even though she annoys him.*

> *He calls her "love" twice. This shows how affectionate he is.*

Not so obvious, this. Remember that the <u>words</u> people use can be really <u>important</u>.

Mini-Essay Questions

On to pointer number two (see p21): "– how he responds to his workplace".

Huge tackle there on the Pittsburg Pointers.

Tackle *The Pointers* One At A Time

About the last two-thirds of the story is about Jerry in his <u>workplace</u>. But the third and fourth pointers are about the employees and customers. Don't talk about them just yet — it makes it easier to <u>structure</u> your work if you talk about the pointers <u>one at a time</u>.

Here, we're just looking for <u>descriptions</u> of how Jerry reacts to the workplace itself.

Bit from the story:

> He positively bounced and skipped the ten minute walk to his shop, so full of energy was he feeling.

You could write this:

> *Jerry is very keen to get to work — he "positively bounced and skipped". This shows how much he likes going to work.*

Bit from the story:

> The door to Jerry's bakery was open, and he could smell the sweet aroma of freshly baking bread. He filled his lungs and beamed with pride...

You could write this:

> *Jerry "beamed with pride" when he gets to his shop. This shows how proud and happy he is with the shop's success.*

Bit from the story:

> As he closed the factory door behind him and surveyed the dozens of workers ... finally, he reflected, all those years of enterprise and hard work had paid off.

You could write this:

> *Looking at his factory, Jerry thinks about how "all those years of enterprise and hard work had paid off". His state of mind here is that he's pleased with his achievements.*

You Can Give Mini-Overviews For The Pointers

It's a good idea to give a short <u>overview</u> for each individual pointer. You could start answering the next pointer ("– the way he treats his employees") like this:

Watch out mate — you've got a mini-over-you.

> *Jerry's state of mind is also revealed by the considerate way in which he treats his employees.*

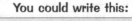

Then you can go on to make specific points about Jerry and his employees.

Writing a <u>linking</u> sentence like this is a <u>clever trick</u>. It proves that you're <u>carefully following</u> the question.

Mini-Essay Questions

Now you can move smoothly on to the third pointer: "– the way Jerry treats his employees".

Just Write Things Down As You Find Them

Read the text again looking for bits about Jerry and his employees. When you find one that is relevant to the question, simply write down what occurs to you.

① *It says that Jerry had given Wayne "a big pay rise". This shows Jerry is generous and wants to share his success.*

> Keep quoting from the story and explaining why the quotes are relevant.

② *The writer describes Jerry as smiling "benevolently" when he's talking to Lisa. This word means he's full of goodwill.*

My bread's got no nose.
How does it smell?
Lovely.

③ *Jerry praises his employees. He tells Wayne the bread "smells wonderful", and he says to Lisa "keep up the good work". He's in a good mood and he's pleased with what his workers are doing.*

There's No Such Thing As Being Too Obvious

Nearly there — just the last pointer to cover. Now we're looking for examples of what Jerry's reactions to his customers tell us about his state of mind.

I've said it before and I'll say it again — don't be scared to state the obvious.

Every day he saw customers' smiling faces in his shop, and it always gave him a warm glow of satisfaction.

Jerry is pleased that his shop is making other people happy — it gives him "a warm glow of satisfaction".

PLEASE DO NOT FEED THE ANIMALS

GLOW WORM OF SATISFACTION

The writer uses the word "considerate" when Jerry puts his arm round the old woman. This shows he's caring.

> Look at the words the writer has chosen. It can tell you a lot.

By giving the old woman a free bun, Jerry again shows his kind and generous state of mind.

Use your fingers — they're handy pointers...

This is a long answer, so there's plenty to learn from it. Always read the handy pointers you get underneath the question, and use them when you go about your answer.

Revision Summary Questions

Da da daa! Revision Summary questions... Alright alright, not the most exciting things, but they ARE the most useful. You can really test your knowledge and make sure you know it all. If there's anything you get stuck on, then go straight back over those pages, and get it learned. Reading test success is all about how you tackle the questions. Pretty obvious really, but that's why this section is so important.

1) How do you find the answers to short questions?
   a) Look in the paragraph where they tell you to look.
   b) Pluck them from thin air.

2) What type of question do you need to pick out individual words for?

3) Writing obvious points in your reading answers will do two of these things. Which ones?
   a) Lose you marks. b) Help you to think of cleverer points. c) Nothing at all.
   d) Waste time. e) Win you marks. f) Make it snow doughnuts in July.

4) What's the big deal about quoting?

5) When you answer a question, you have to pick out all the relevant bits that are to do with the question. Can you write about other things as well?

6) How can you start your answers?

7) How do you back up your points?

8) When the question has handy pointers underneath, how many of them should you write about?

9) 90% of Columbian fruit bats think that authors just throw words together at random. Are they right? If not, what should your approach to it be?

10) Is it better to talk about the pointers
    a) kind of mixed in together, b) just one at a time, or c) in Latin?
    Why?

11) What happens when you're being too obvious? ← (This is a trick question.)

The 'red ing' test...

Give Reasons

This is a bargain basement of a section — it'll really help your marks on the Reading paper and the Shakespeare question. That's excellent value. And it grates carrots too.

Give Reasons from the bit of Writing

Where did he come from?

From the writing.

You have to give reasons for what you say — examples from the passage you've read that show where your answer comes from.

If you don't give reasons, the examiners can't tell if you know what you're talking about. Examples show you haven't got it right by a lucky fluke.

> *The women at the banjo club aren't very friendly. In fact they're downright rude.*

...but this answer gives a reason from the writing to justify every point it makes. That's loads better.

This answer doesn't give any reasons...

> *The women at the banjo club aren't very friendly — they ignore Mrs Icenoggle when she tries to say hello. In fact they're downright rude — they look at her, but then they start talking among themselves.*

Every Time you make a Point — give an Example

It's easy to forget to give examples from the bit of writing you've read. You'd think because the examiner knows what you've read, they'd easily get what you're talking about.

But that's the road to losing loads and loads of marks. They want you to refer to the writing — as if they didn't know it. Drum this simple rule into your head:

> Every time you make a point, back it up with an example.

Hey bear — gimme some cover while I'm making this point.

No fear, partner — I'll be your back-up. Those guys don't stand a chance!

Never forget your back-up

Give reasons — and currants, and sultanas...

The sure-fire way to get good marks in these English SATs is to make sure you put loads of examples in your answer. Reasons and examples — nothing else is going to do.

Using your Own Words

When you link your answer to the piece you've read, use <u>new words</u> to show you understand it.

Don't just Copy Bits Out

When you give your answer, <u>don't</u> just <u>copy out</u> what the piece says word for word.
Any old fool can do that, so it <u>doesn't prove</u> to the examiner that you've <u>understood</u> it.

Here's part of a story:

> "Hello," Mrs Icenoggle began to say. But the sour-faced woman turned away and started to talk to her companions.

> *When Mrs Icenoggle began to say hello, the sour-faced woman turned away and started to talk to her companions.*

No stealing the words straight from the text.

This isn't a good way to talk about the story.

It uses all the <u>same words</u> as the story — it <u>doesn't</u> show that you <u>understand</u>.

Don't be a Copy cat

Put your Reason In Your Own Words

Prove you've understood what you've read — use <u>your own words</u>.

Banjo Club

Hello.....Hello.....

I wonder what's goat into them?

> *The woman ignored Mrs Icenoggle when she tried to say hello.*

All I've done here is say what happened <u>in my own words</u> — but it proves I know what's going on.

Be careful you don't get confused between <u>referring</u> to a story and <u>quoting</u> from it.
<u>Quoting</u> means <u>copying bits out</u> word for word and putting <u>speech marks</u> round them.
There's more on quoting on the next page.

Remember — when you're giving a reason <u>always use your own words</u>.

Tracing teeth marks? — don't copy 'bites' out...

You know you have to give <u>reasons</u> and <u>explanations</u> in your answer and that means you've gotta <u>use your own words</u>. So kick-start your brain and say it <u>your way</u> — don't just copy it.

How to Quote

You can make plenty of good points in your answer, but you won't get all the marks if you don't stick in loads of <u>lovely quotes</u> too.

Quote, Quote, Quote — And Quote Some More

Examiners <u>love</u> you to quote bits from the writing. It'll get you <u>masses</u> of extra marks.

Quotes are great because they show <u>exactly</u> which bit you've got your answer from.

Quoting <u>isn't</u> the same as stealing words from the story or article you've read. There's a <u>massive difference</u>...

Quotes Have Speech Marks

<u>Speech marks</u> make all the difference. They show that <u>you're quoting</u>, not just stealing words. Without speech marks you'll lose marks.

 66 Everything inside the speech marks is a quote. It has to be word for word what the text says. **99**

> "Hello," Mrs Icenoggle began to say. But the sour-faced woman turned away and started to talk to her companions.
>
> "Did you go to Iona's party last weekend?" she asked.
>
> All the other women glanced briefly at Mrs Icenoggle. "I certainly did," replied one of them, "and I don't like the way Iona has redecorated her toilet."
>
> Mrs Icenoggle, who had no idea who Iona was, stood helplessly by the doorway...

The writer describes one of the women as "sour-faced" That makes us think she's not a nice person.

Speech Marks

The <u>speech marks</u> show that you're <u>quoting</u>. When you quote, make sure it's copied <u>word for word</u>.

Keep it short and sweet.

 Iona's

The women at the banjo club are rude. They talk among themselves even though they all know Mrs Icenoggle is there — "all the other women glanced briefly at Mrs Icenoggle".

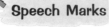 Speech Marks

Quote early, quote often...

Remember — <u>copying</u> = <u>bad</u>, but <u>quoting</u> = <u>good</u> (sounds daft, I know, but it's true). If you only learn one other thing about quoting, learn this: Quotes always have to have speech marks.

Explain the Quote

It's no good just sticking a quote down on its own. That doesn't prove anything.
You have to make sure you <u>explain why you're using a quote</u>.

 You can Put the Explanation <u>Before</u> the Quote

Here I've used a quote to <u>back up a reason</u> I've just given.

> The answer <u>makes a point</u> — it says the women are rude.

> Then there's <u>a reason to back it up</u> — the women talk among themselves even though they know Mrs Icenoggle is there.

> Now there's a quote from the text. The quote <u>proves the point</u> that the other women all know Mrs Icenoggle is there.

The women at the banjo club are rude. They talk among themselves even though they all know Mrs Icenoggle is there —
"all three other women glanced briefly at Mrs Icenoggle".

Ouch!
this is bloomin hot!

Egg's pain

 You can Give the Quote <u>First</u>

This is an example of the <u>second</u> kind of way to use a quote.

A rooster laying an egg?
Eggs-plain that one!

The writer describes one of the women as *"sour-faced"*.
That makes us think she's not a nice person.

> This time the quote gets in there first.
> Then the answer explains why it's relevant to answering the question.

> If I just wrote this bit, I wouldn't get as many marks. The examiner needs to know why you think the quote is important.

The writer describes one of the women as *"sour-faced"*.

Always <u>explain why</u> the quote is relevant.

It <u>doesn't matter</u> what order you do it in — make a point, then back it up with a quote — or quote then explain. The important thing is that you <u>always explain why</u> your quote helps you <u>answer</u> the question.

Eggs — plain, fried or scrambled...

<u>You</u> know why you've chosen your quote. The Examiners <u>won't know</u> — so you need to <u>tell</u> them.

Keeping Quotes Short

<u>Don't</u> think that you'll get better marks for using <u>longer</u> quotes.
You <u>won't</u>. In fact you'll <u>lose</u> marks for it.

Never Quote More than A Few Words...

Follow the path of few words you must.

Quotes are to show that <u>you've read the bit of text</u> you're talking about.
You usually only need to quote a few words.

> Buckingham accepts that he is getting what he deserves:
> *"This, this All Souls' Day to my fearful soul*
> *Is the determined respite of my wrongs:*
> *That high All-seer which I dallied with*
> *Hath turned my feigned prayer on my head*
> *And given in earnest what I begged in jest."*
> *Act 5, Scene 1, 18-22*

> Buckingham accepts that he is getting what he deserves:
> *"This, this All Souls' Day to my fearful soul*
> *Is the determined respite of my wrongs"*
> *Act 5, Scene 1, 18-19*

This quote is <u>far too long</u>. It <u>doesn't</u> make the answer better, and it uses up precious <u>time</u> that you could spend writing something else.

This quote is much better. It's <u>short</u> and it has everything you need to <u>make your point</u>.

Far too long!

Try to quote using the <u>fewest</u> number of words you can. Don't be afraid just to quote a <u>single word</u> if it's <u>enough</u> to make your point.

Short & to the Point

... But Do It Often

Your answer should be <u>full</u> of <u>short</u> quotes <u>backing up</u> your points.

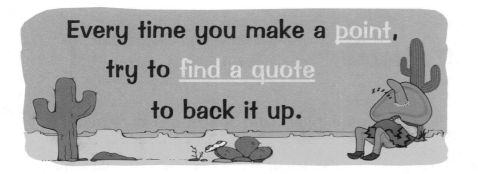

Every time you make a point, try to find a quote to back it up.

Hey Pedro, Do you get my POINT?

You might not always be able to, but <u>always try</u>. Your answers will be much better with loads of <u>good quotes</u>.

Phew-urgh words are better...

You <u>don't</u> need to quote vast chunks of writing, just the bit that makes the point. Be economical.

Revision Summary Questions

Quoting is dead important — "Quote me baby one more time," as Britney Spears once said... Maybe not. Anyhow, there's no way to get all the marks you want, without a clear and thorough understanding of the whole of this section. Test yourself on these questions, and go over the section until you can do them all.

1) What do you have to do to back up every point you make?

2) When you give your answer, is it OK to write your reasons in exactly the same words as the piece of writing uses?

3) If it's not OK, why not? What should you do instead?

4) When can you copy the words exactly?

5) How do you show that something's a quote?

6) Is using quotes   a) a bad idea,   b) against the law in Stockholm, or   c) a great idea?

7) What are the two important ways of giving a reason and explaining it with a quote?

8) What are the rules on how long a quote should be?

9) How often should you use quotes?

What You Have To Do

On the Shakespeare paper you have to answer a question about the set scenes you're doing. This section is full of tips on how to answer the Shakespeare question well. So get stuck in. There are two big things you have to do to get marks.

1) Show You Understand What's Going On

Don't worry — it's not just you who reads Shakespeare and thinks "aargh — what does it mean?"

What's going on? / I'm not sure. That's half the battle.

The examiners know that — and you'll get plenty of marks just for showing that you know what's happening.

To show you understand the bit of the play, you need to:

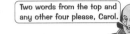

Two words from the top and any other four please, Carol.

> 1) Write about the way the characters are feeling.
> 2) Write about Shakespeare's choice of words.

2) Use Quotes To Back Up Your Points

Remember I banged on about how important quoting is in your reading paper — well, it's just as important in the Shakespeare paper — if not more so. You have to quote.

If you talk about the play without using bags of quotes, they won't be convinced that you really know your stuff.

Thou liest, most ignorant monster.

A plague a'both your houses!

I need help — he's got quotes to back him up.

Make sure you stick your quotes in speech marks, and only use the exact words that Shakespeare uses.

And — You'll Do Better if You Write Well

1) You don't get marks for writing flashy English on the set scenes question. But if you write badly the examiners won't be able to understand what you're saying, and that'll make them grumpy and stingy with marks.

2) Don't forget to write in paragraphs. Every time you want to talk about a new idea, start a new paragraph.

3) Here's the tough one — try to sound interested in the play, even if you don't like it. Show the examiners that you're keen by using lots of interesting words and phrases in your answer.

Writer manages to sit — Shakespeare SAT success...

Your three tips for Shakespeare success — show you get what's going on, use lots of quotes from the play, and write clearly in proper paragraphs, with some interesting words. Not much, then...

What You Get in the Exam

To cure people who are scared of spiders, they show them lots of spiders. If you've got exam-phobia, look at this page — you'll know what to expect in the exam, and it won't freak you out.

You have to Write About your Set Scenes

You will study one Shakespeare play for your exam.

You will be told the set scenes for the play you're studying. The set scenes are important because your exam question will focus on them.

> You have to write about the set scenes in detail in the exam and show you know them inside-out.

You have to know about the rest of the play as well — but not in as much detail.

Here's How the Shakespeare Question Works

1) Bits from the scenes will be printed on the exam paper, and a good job too — you can remind yourself what happens and get quotes for your essay. They'll probably give you one whole scene and a bit from another one.

2) Read the scenes through before you try answering the question.

3) Keep looking back to them as you write your answer.

4) This is what the actual question will look like:

Maybe Alonso's wacky nephew from Brisbane should turn up...

Stick to these bits of the play in your answer. Write about both or you'll lose a ton of marks.

The Tempest
Act 2 Scene 1, lines 98-131
Act 3 Scene 3, lines 1-102

In these scenes, Alonso faces some disturbing situations.

What do Alonso's reactions to his problems reveal about his character?

Support your ideas by referring to both of the extracts which are printed on the following pages.

This is the actual question (obviously). Don't write about whatever comes into your head — answer the question.

This means "back up everything you say with quotes". They mean it. You'll get twice as many marks if you do.

Make quick notes — play a trumpet on Concorde...

OK, here we go. Once you've got started, it's not so scary. Read the questions and the bit of the play carefully, use the hints you're given, and above all, don't panic. Then you'll be fine.

Preparing Your Answer

There are two things you've got to do in the test <u>before</u> you put pen to paper — <u>work out what the question wants</u>, and <u>plan</u> your answer. Seems like a bit of a <u>hassle</u> but it's totally <u>worth it</u>.

Check Exactly *What the Task is* Asking For

It's a good idea to <u>start</u> by <u>reading through</u> the bits from the scenes.
Now have a good look at exactly what the <u>question</u> is asking you to do.

These are the <u>most important words</u> in the question. This is what you'd have to <u>write about</u>.

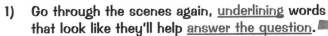

> **What do we learn about the character of Romeo from these scenes?**
>
> Support your ideas with references to the following extracts.

1) Go through the scenes again, <u>underlining</u> words that look like they'll help <u>answer the question</u>.
2) For this one you'd underline <u>anything</u> that reveals something about Romeo's character.
3) Then go through <u>again</u> looking for any <u>less obvious</u> bits about Romeo.

> He jests at scars that never felt a wound.
> But soft, what light through yonder window...

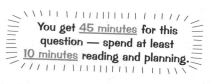

You get <u>45 minutes</u> for this question — spend at least <u>10 minutes</u> reading and planning.

Plan *Your Essay*

Before you start writing <u>MAKE A PLAN</u>.

1) It'll help you <u>get your ideas straight</u>.

2) You can arrange your points in a <u>sensible order</u>.

3) It should mean you <u>don't forget</u> anything important.

This essay is all about <u>Romeo</u>, so make notes on <u>anything</u> from the scenes you think tells us something about Romeo.

Write down any <u>comments</u> you've got about each one.

Find some <u>good quotes</u> to back up your points.

Decide on the best <u>order</u> to write about your points.

Romeo's character

1. *He's very determined* *He continues to pursue Juliet, even though their families are enemies.*
   "Is she a Capulet?
   O dear account! My life is my foe's debt."

3. 2. *He is well respected* *He is allowed to stay at the Capulet banquet.*
   "And to say truth, Verona brags of him
   To be a virtuous and well-governed youth."
   He is also considered to be brave.
   "Nay, he will answer the letter's master, how he dares, being dared."

2. 3. *He's reckless* *He breaks into the Capulet mansion over a wall. Later he kills Tybalt, and then Paris.*

My essay blossomed — I plant it well...

It really is <u>ultra-important</u> to make sure you know what you're supposed to write about before you start. If you don't do what the task says, you won't get the <u>marks</u>. That's the simple truth.

Writing Your Answer

All the questions are different, but there are a few basic points that'll help you do any of them.

Watch your Paragraphs, Sentences and Spelling

It's no good understanding the play if you don't write well.
Here are some tips on impressing the examiner with what you write.

1) Think about what you want to say, and make sure your sentences are good and clear.

2) Every time you make a new point, start a new paragraph.

3) Link your points together well.

Use phrases like "Another way that Shakespeare creates tension is..."

4) Take care with those spellings.

And watch your step, too.

Don't forget to Quote

It all hinges on this...

Quoting is the key. If you don't quote, you won't get the marks — it really is that simple.

Remember, the whole purpose of quoting is to back up a point you've made.

Here's an example...

> Romeo is clearly impatient to marry Juliet. He has climbed the high walls into the Capulet mansion and has risked being caught and killed by the guards to see her in Act 2 scene 2. He wants them to promise to marry each other, even though this is the first time they have properly met.
>
> "JULIET   What satisfaction canst thou have tonight?
> ROMEO   Th'exchange of thy love's faithful vow for mine."
>
> Act 2 Scene 2 lines 126-127.

If you're quoting more than one line, put the quote in a separate paragraph.

Say where the quote comes from. Give the act, scene and line numbers.

Make a point, give a quote and explain why you've used the quote.

Cheap plumbers — they give the best quotes...

In every single paragraph, aim to QUOTE. You'd have to be some sort of nutter to forget to quote after reading this page. If you quote well in your SAT, you're onto a winner.

Tricky Play Terms

You'll just have to <u>learn</u> these words, I'm afraid. Without them it'll never quite make sense.

A Play is divided into Acts and Scenes

The play is divided into <u>five</u> big sections, called <u>acts</u>. Each act is like an <u>episode</u> of a TV serial — lots of things happen in it, but it's only <u>part</u> of the whole thing.

Each act is made up of <u>smaller</u> sections called <u>scenes</u>. Scenes are just a way of <u>breaking up</u> the story. A new scene starts when time has passed or the story moves to a different place.

"Act" and "Scene" are two words you're likely to have to bandy about in the SAT, so make sure you know what they mean.

In the SAT, you'll probably get a question on <u>one whole scene</u> and a <u>bit</u> from <u>another scene</u>.

Shakespeare wrote Three Kinds of Play

Shakespeare wrote <u>three</u> main kinds of play. You can <u>impress</u> the examiner by using these words in your SAT, so make sure you know what they mean.

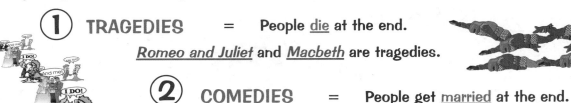

① **TRAGEDIES** = People <u>die</u> at the end.

Romeo and Juliet and *Macbeth* are tragedies.

② **COMEDIES** = People get <u>married</u> at the end.

Much Ado About Nothing and *The Tempest* are comedies.

③ **HISTORIES** = These are based on <u>real history</u>.

Richard III and *Henry V* are histories.

Characters are the People in the Play

There are a few <u>main</u> characters in each play that you have to know all about. There are also loads of <u>minor</u> characters who don't do anything very important. For example, in Romeo and Juliet:

These three are important characters

Romeo   Juliet   Mercutio

Burn the people in the play — Char-actors...

Seems a bit like a list of random facts about Shakespeare's plays to me. They are <u>important</u> random facts, though. Don't let yourself get <u>acts</u> and <u>scenes</u> mixed up, and remember those <u>three types</u> of play. You'll be able to impress the examiner with them, and that means a better grade.

More Play Features

A lot of the things you'll find <u>odd</u> when you read a scene from Shakespeare are there because it's a <u>play</u>. Learn what it all means now and you won't be <u>confused</u> in the Exam.

<u>Plays</u> are written to be Acted

This is a <u>massive</u>, <u>huge difference</u> between a Shakespeare play and a novel or short story. A novel tells a story by <u>describing</u> it to you. A play tells a story by <u>showing</u> it to you.

You <u>don't</u> get any long describing bits in a play. The actors show the audience what's going on by the <u>way</u> they say their lines — laughing, shouting or whatever — as well as <u>what</u> they say.

The audience <u>don't</u> have the <u>playscript</u> in front of them, so the <u>actors</u> have to do all the <u>work</u>.

Four years at drama school, then the RSC... And STILL we actors have to do all the work...

In the Exam, <u>you</u> have to do all the work. You have to work out what's going on <u>just</u> by reading the scenes.

Sometimes Characters <u>Talk To Themselves</u>

This seems <u>strange</u>. People in real life don't <u>usually</u> talk to themselves — if they did, pretty soon you'd start to <u>worry</u> about them.

Characters in plays do this so the audience can hear what they're <u>thinking</u> and <u>feeling</u>. They're really talking for the <u>benefit</u> of the audience.

Talking to yourself — crazy.

| TRINCULO | Here's neither bush nor shrub to bear off any weather at all, and another storm brewing; I hear it sing i'th'wind. Yond same black cloud, yond huge one, looks like a foul bombard that would shed his liquor. If it should thunder as it did before, I know not where to hide my head. |

Trinculo hasn't spotted Caliban yet. He thinks he's on his own.

Trinculo's not actually talking to anyone — he's just wondering to himself where he's going to shelter from the storm.

Trinculo is <u>thinking</u> these things. People don't usually think out loud, but you wouldn't know what was going on in Trinculo's head if he didn't <u>tell</u> you. Shakespeare makes him say it <u>out loud</u>.

Is this a badger which I see before me?

Sometimes characters say thoughts <u>aloud</u> when <u>other</u> characters are on the stage. When you see the word <u>[Aside]</u>, that's what's happening — the <u>audience</u> can hear, but the <u>other</u> characters can't.

Plays for insects — written to bee acted...

It seems pretty <u>weird</u> to me. They were all written to be <u>acted on stage</u>, but you have to read them — there's no one to <u>act it out</u> in the Exam, so you have to understand it all from the <u>script</u>.

More Play Features

When you <u>read</u> Shakespeare plays, it helps if you <u>imagine</u> what would be happening if they were being said by <u>actors</u> on stage. Luckily, you get some <u>clues</u> as to what would be going on.

Stage Directions *Give a Few Clues*

Stage directions show the actors what to do, when to come in and when to leave the stage.

> "Enter" is a stage direction. It tells the person playing Lady Capulet to enter.

> The character name is here to tell you who's speaking. So it's Lady Capulet who's saying these lines.

> Exeunt is a daft word. All it means is that more than one person leaves the stage.

[Enter Lady Capulet]

LADY CAPULET What, are you busy, ho? Need you my help?

JULIET No, madam, we have culled such necessaries
As are behoveful for our state tomorrow.
So please you, let me now be left alone,
And let the Nurse this night sit up with you,
For I am sure you have your hands full all,
In this so sudden business.

LADY CAPULET   Good night.
Get thee to bed and rest, for thou hast need.

[Exeunt Lady Capulet and Nurse]

Stage directions are <u>great</u>, because they tell you the basics of what's <u>happening</u> on stage. Always read them when you read a play.

The Director *Decides the Rest*

Sometimes the stage directions <u>tell</u> the actors how to say their lines. More often though, the <u>director</u> has to work out how the actors should say the lines — sadly, angrily or whatever.

OK, Prospero — now let's try the speech again, but this time hopping on the other foot.

The <u>director</u> decides what the actors should do to <u>help</u> the audience <u>understand</u> what's going on.

You might be asked in the SAT to imagine that <u>you're</u> a director, and you have to <u>tell</u> the actors how to act in that scene.

Unfortunately, you don't have a director to help you in the exam — you've got to figure it <u>all</u> out for yourself, from the <u>words</u>.

Past the curtains, on your right — stage directions...

Right, so that's what <u>stage directions</u> are, then. Use them to help you imagine how the actors would be <u>saying</u> the words and what they'd be <u>doing</u> on the stage. Don't forget: exeunt = exit.

Other Strange Things

Some of the things the characters do seem really <u>strange</u> to us. Remember, though, that it was all written <u>400 years</u> ago — and Shakespeare chose some very <u>odd</u> settings.

The Character Names Look Odd

Don't be put off by the fact that some of the characters have <u>funny</u> looking names. Shakespeare set some of his plays in <u>foreign</u> countries and gave the characters foreign names.

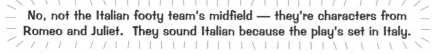

Mercutio	Tybalt	Benvolio

On the head Mercutio...

Pronto-pronto Benvolio!

Man-on Tybalt...

No, not the Italian footy team's midfield — they're characters from Romeo and Juliet. They sound Italian because the play's set in Italy.

Ariel

Sometimes the character <u>names</u> are supposed to be <u>funny</u> or <u>represent something</u>. Don't worry if you don't get them or find them <u>side-splittingly hilarious</u>. People's sense of <u>humour</u> and the <u>meaning</u> of names in Shakespeare's day were <u>different</u>. As long as you <u>know</u> the names, it doesn't really matter what they <u>mean</u> — but since you asked Ariel is a name often associated with <u>magic</u> and legend.

Life Was Different Back Then

Remember that things have <u>changed</u> a lot since Shakespeare's day — plus Shakespeare set some of his plays even further back in the past — when things seem <u>even odder</u>.

In The Tempest, there are magic spells and fairies who can appear in different forms. People believed in magic in Shakespeare's day more than they do now, so this wouldn't have seemed as odd to them as it does to us.

In Romeo and Juliet, there is a long running and violent feud between the Capulet and Montague families. That isn't so unusual — but getting married at 13 and then pretending to take poison and die so you can run off with the bloke you married three hours ago isn't really that common today.

It's easy to get <u>put off</u> by how freaky some Shakespeare seems. Remember that the world Shakespeare writes about is radically <u>different</u> from our world — then the plays will be <u>a doddle</u>.

Fairies and magic — that spells trouble...

OK, you didn't need me to tell you that Shakespeare's odd. But remember, it's often just the way things were back then. And be thankful that the Duke of Milan isn't a cheeky wizard any more...

Revision Summary Questions

As if reading and writing tests weren't bad enough, you're stuck with doing Shakespeare as well.
Shakespeare can be really intimidating — especially if you're not used to it. The language is old and
funny looking and often it doesn't seem to make any sense at all. But read this section and have a
go, and you'll be able to pick up bits of it. And then some more bits, and some more...
So make sure you've learned this section well enough to answer all these questions.

1)   What is the three-point plan to Shakespeare SAT success?

2)   You'll get good marks simply by showing you understand what's going on. True or false?

3)   How important is it to use lots of quotes?

4)   Only one of these statements is true. Which one?
   a) You have to understand every single word of Shakespeare to do well in your SAT.
   b) You don't have to understand it all — you only have to know roughly what's happening.
   c) Shakespeare's plays were written in the 1960s by a Surbiton chartered accountant.

5)   Will the exam questions always be about your set scenes?

6)   If the question asks you to write about two scenes, is it ok just to talk about one of them?

7)   What two things should you do in the exam before you start writing your answer?

8)   What kind of stuff should you write in your plan?

9)   When should you start a new paragraph?

10) What's the point of quoting?
   a) To fill up space when you can't think of anything to write.
   b) To back up what you're saying and get you more marks.
   c) Good question. There's no point.

11) When should you put a quote in a separate paragraph?

12) What should you put after a quote to show where it's come from in the play?

13) What's an Act?

14) And a Scene?

15) What are the three kinds of plays that Shakespeare wrote?

16) What happens at the end of a tragedy?

17) What kind of play is Romeo and Juliet?

18) Give an example of a major character in one of the plays.

19) Why aren't there any long descriptive bits in the plays?

20) Why do Shakespeare's characters sometimes talk to themselves?

21) What does [Aside] mean?

22) What does [Exeunt] mean?

23) Why is it useful to read the stage directions?

24) What does a director do?

25) Why do some of Shakespeare's characters have odd-sounding names?

26) Why do some of the things that happen in Shakespeare's plays seem strange to us?

So, what's all the fuss about shaking spears for anyway?

Shakespeare's Language

It doesn't matter if you think Shakespeare is <u>weird</u> or <u>boring</u>. The important thing is it's <u>not impossible</u>. This section's here to make it all less scary and more doable.

It's Weird — but it gets Easier With Practice

Once you get used to the annoying weird language, Shakespeare is perfectly doable. Remember, you <u>don't</u> have to like it, but you <u>do</u> have to <u>do an Exam</u> on it.

And it's not <u>THAT</u> boring. The plays have <u>stories</u> full of <u>violence</u>, <u>villains</u>, <u>murder</u>, <u>love</u>, <u>double-crossing</u> and <u>betrayal</u>.

The key thing about Shakespeare is getting to grips with the <u>funny language</u>. It's not easy, but you can <u>learn</u> how to do it. <u>Practise</u> reading your scenes — the more you read them, the <u>easier</u> they'll be to understand.

You Don't Have To Understand Every Word

That's right — if you read it loads and there are still bits you look at and go "<u>huh</u>?", don't worry. It's OK. As long as you've got the basic <u>idea</u> of what's going on, you'll be fine.

Take a look at this — it's the kind of question you'll get in the exam.

My, my, what a scene.

But I don't understand it.

| How important is the use of magic in Prospero's plans? |

This tests if you've <u>understood</u> what Prospero is trying to do, and how he uses magic to do it. If you show you understand basically <u>what's going on</u>, you <u>don't</u> need to explain the meaning of every single word.

Don't look at your exam paper and have an attack of the <u>wobblies</u> because there's a tiny bit of the <u>scene</u> you don't understand.

You don't need to understand <u>every single word</u>. You need to understand <u>what's going on</u> in the scene you get in the Exam.

Oil gauge, pressure gauge — what's a lan guage...

Shakespeare <u>isn't</u> that boring if you understand the <u>weird language</u>. It gets easier with practice, and in any case you don't have to understand <u>all</u> of it — as long as you get the basic idea.

Shakespeare's Language

When you first read a Shakespeare play, it seems like you'll never <u>understand</u> a word. <u>Don't give up</u>, though. The <u>more</u> you read the play, the <u>easier</u> it gets and the more <u>you'll get it</u>.

The Language *Isn't* Everyday *Modern English*

<u>Shakespeare</u> wasn't trying to <u>confuse</u> you by using <u>funny language</u> — believe it or not, when he was alive people <u>really did use</u> those strange words. He wrote his plays <u>about 400 years ago</u>.

See if this speech from *The Tempest* is any easier to understand after you've read the "translation".

> In the past, Alonso betrayed Prospero when Antonio robbed him of his title of Duke of Milan. Prospero was set adrift at sea. Now, after making sure Alonso and his followers have a horrible time, Prospero finally reveals himself and prepares to forgive them.

Here's what's in the play...

PROSPERO   Behold, Sir King,
The wronged Duke of Milan, Prospero.
For more assurance that a living prince
Does now speak to thee, I embrace thy body,
And to thee and thy company I bid
A hearty welcome.
ALONSO   Whe'er thou be'st he or no,
Or some enchanted trifle to abuse me,
As late I have been, I not know. Thy pulse
Beats as of flesh and blood, and, since I saw thee,
Th'affliction of my mind amends, with which,
I fear, a madness held me.

...and this is roughly what it means.

"Look, it's me, Prospero, the bloke who was robbed of being Duke of Milan. To prove it really is me, I'm going to give you a hug. A big welcome to you and your mates."

"Whether it really is you, or some weird magic trick to torture me like the others, I don't know. You've got a pulse just like a real person. Since you appeared, I've felt a lot better, and I don't feel like I'm going mad any more."

Some Sentences are in a *Funny Order*

People <u>swapped</u> round the <u>order of words</u> a lot more in those days. If you <u>jiggle</u> the word order around a bit you can usually work out what it means.

Where the devil should this Romeo be? Came he not home tonight?

= Where the devil is Romeo? Didn't he come home last night?

Funny Sentences — by order of drunken judges...

"But I don't understand a word of it!" I hear you cry. Don't panic. Keep reading it and try to pick out a bit here and there. You only need to know what's going on — not every word.

Shakespeare's Language

Shakespeare writes a lot in <u>verse</u>, or <u>poetry</u> — and he often uses lots of words to say something <u>simple</u>. This page will help you to <u>make sense</u> of what you're reading.

Don't *Stop Reading At The* End Of The Line

When you read verse, it's <u>tempting to stop</u> at the <u>end</u> of a line. <u>Don't</u> — unless there's a full stop, the sentence carries on. It makes <u>no sense</u> if you <u>pause</u> at the end of every single line. Try reading this extract from *The Tempest*.

ALONSO	You cram these words into mine ears against The stomach of my sense. Would I had never Married my daughter there, for, coming thence, My son is lost, and, in my rate, she too, Who is so far from Italy removed I ne'er again shall see her. O thou mine heir Of Naples and of Milan, what strange fish Hath made his meal on thee?

If you stop at the end of each line, this makes no sense. It would sound like: "O thou mine heir. Of Naples and of Milan, what strange fish. Hath made his meal on thee?"

It'll make a lot more sense if you read it all as one sentence: "Oh thou mine heir of Naples and Milan, what strange fish hath made his meal on thee?"

Don't pause at the end of lines when you're reading Shakespeare — <u>pause</u> when you get to <u>punctuation</u>, the <u>commas</u> and <u>full stops</u>, like in other writing. It'll make <u>much more sense</u>.

Characters Use An *Awful Lot Of Words*

One thing you're <u>bound</u> to notice about Shakespeare is that the characters <u>don't half go on</u>. They use an <u>awful lot</u> of words to say something <u>simple</u>.

Have <u>another look</u> at that speech by <u>Alonso</u>, from *The Tempest*. He talks for ages but all he's saying is <u>basically</u> this:

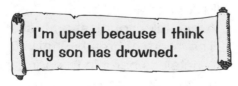

I'm upset because I think my son has drowned.

The way the speeches are so <u>long-winded</u> might be a bit <u>irritating</u>, but it's <u>the key</u> to getting <u>good marks</u>. You have to talk <u>about how</u> Shakespeare uses this <u>flowery language</u> to show what <u>characters</u> are <u>thinking</u> and <u>feeling</u>.

Shakespeare was probably paid by the word...

Make sure that you don't pause at the end of each and every line — look at the <u>punctuation</u> instead. And bear in mind that characters use loads of words for ideas that are basically simple.

Shakespeare's Language

You'd have to be as nutty as a fruitcake to walk around speaking in poetry. I don't do it (much).
Understand why Shakespeare wrote like that and you've got a head start in the SAT.

Only The Posh Characters Talk In Poetry

In Shakespeare's day, writers always made their posher characters talk in verse — while
the more common characters talked in normal, everyday prose (like, not poetry).

NURSE   I will tell her, sir, that you do protest — which, as I
take it, is a gentlemanlike offer.

ROMEO   Bid her devise
Some means to come to shrift this afternoon;
And there she shall at Friar Lawrence' cell
Be shrived and married. Here is for thy pains.

In this scene from
'Romeo and Juliet',
Romeo talks in verse, but
Nurse (an ordinary woman)
talks in prose.

If Shakespeare had made
Romeo talk in prose, it
would have sounded daft to
audiences at the time —
kinda like a BBC newsreader
talking in cockney slang.

Posh characters talk in fancy poetry. Sometimes poorer
characters talk in verse too, but usually only when they're
spouting about big ideas.

Sometimes the posher characters talk in prose — like Romeo,
Mercutio and Benvolio in Act 2, Scene 4. Urgh — confusing. It
doesn't mean they've suddenly become lower class — it means
they're bantering with each other in a casual, chummy way.

Some Posh Spices

Poetry Makes It Easier To Sound Grand

Shakespeare uses poetry to make what he's writing about fancier. Check it out:

This is Romeo's death
speech. He's about to
take poison in
order to die with Juliet,
who he thinks is
already dead.

ROMEO   And shake the yoke of inauspicious stars
From this world-wearied flesh. Eyes, look your last!
Arms, take your last embrace! And, lips, O you
The doors of breath, seal with a righteous kiss
A dateless bargain to engrossing death!
Come, bitter conduct, come, unsavoury guide!
Thou desperate pilot, now at once run on
The dashing rocks thy seasick weary bark!
Here's to my love!

Going from bad to poor to verse...

I reckon it's ridiculous. But people didn't think it was ridiculous then. Shakespeare wrote in verse
when a posh character was speaking, or when he wanted his writing to sound more awesome.
And remember — Nine times out of ten when prose crops up it means someone common is talking.

Shakespeare's Language

It's easy to lose marks in your SAT because you feel <u>intimidated</u> by the <u>bizarre language</u> in Shakespeare. Don't be — the <u>weird stuff</u> is there for a <u>reason</u>, and it's nothing to be scared of.

Rhymed _Verse Sounds_ Even Grander

Shakespeare's verse <u>doesn't always rhyme</u> — the important thing is that the words fit a <u>rhythm</u>.

But sometimes Shakespeare does use rhyme to create a <u>special effect</u>. He uses rhyme to sound <u>even grander</u> than usual.

> Honour, riches, marriage-blessing,
> Long continuance, and increasing,
> Hourly joys be still upon you!
> Juno sings her blessings on you.

The goddesses in _**The Tempest**_ speak in rhyme. It makes them sound wise and knowledgeable.

The rhyming final lines of <u>Romeo and Juliet</u> sum up the tragedy of the story perfectly.

> Go hence, to have more talk of these sad things.
> Some shall be pardoned, and some punishèd,
> For never was a story of more woe
> Than this of Juliet and her Romeo.

Don't Worry About The Funny _Old Words_

<u>Don't be put off</u> — it's normally pretty <u>obvious</u> what they mean.

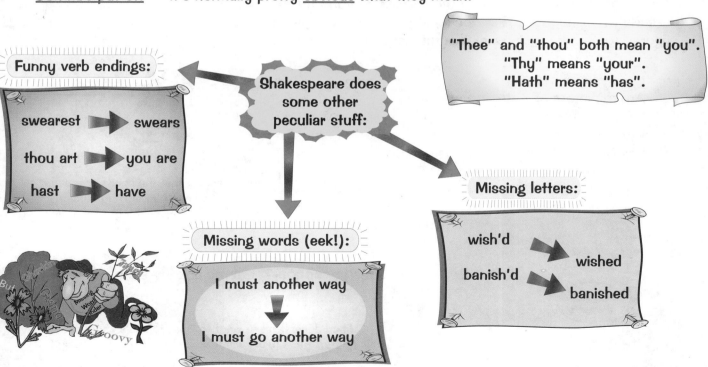

"Thee" and "thou" both mean "you".
"Thy" means "your".
"Hath" means "has".

Shakespeare does some other peculiar stuff:

Funny verb endings:

swearest ➡ swears

thou art ➡ you are

hast ➡ have

Missing words (eek!):

I must another way
⬇
I must go another way

Missing letters:

wish'd ➡ wished

banish'd ➡ banished

Do the opposite in song — inverse in verse...

When Shakespeare makes his verses rhyme, you can almost bet money it's to sound even <u>grander</u>. And don't turn your nose up at the strange old words — replace them in your mind with normal ones.

Shakespeare's Language

Think back to the writing section when I told you about ways of <u>comparing</u> things —
Shakespeare does this <u>loads</u>, and you'll get <u>great</u> marks for writing about how he does it.

You Have To Write About Comparisons

Shakespeare <u>loves</u> comparing things to other things.
Sometimes he'll give you a helping hand by making it really <u>obvious</u> that he's doing this.

> I mean, sir, in delay
> We waste our lights in vain, like lamps by day.

The word "like" shows you Shakespeare is making a comparison. Here Mercutio in *Romeo and Juliet* is complaining that he and Romeo are wasting time and should get a move on.

Sometimes it's a bit less obvious — and you've got to be <u>sharp</u> to notice he's doing it.

> ANTONIO   Which, of he or Adrian, for a good wager,
>   first begins to crow?
> SEBASTIAN   The old cock.
> ANTONIO   The cock'rel.

In this extract from *The Tempest*, Antonio and Sebastian are making fun out of
Gonzalo and Adrian by comparing their conversation to cockerels crowing.

The Characters Seem To Speak In Riddles

This is really <u>annoying</u> at first. The characters don't mean
exactly what they say. But you'll get great marks if you can
<u>figure</u> it out and <u>explain</u> what they actually do mean.

Every morning a man gets a lift to the 12th floor of the building, gets out and walks the last 4 floors to his office on the 16th floor. Why?

> I and my fellows
> Are ministers of Fate, the elements
> Of whom your swords are tempered may as well
> Wound the loud winds, or with bemocked-at stabs
> Kill the still-closing waters, as diminish
> One dowl that's in my plume.

Ariel is saying that the spirits are made
of air and can't be hurt by human
weapons — it would be like trying to
cut the sea in half or stab the wind.

The King will never get my riddle.

> CALIBAN   How does thy honour? Let me lick thy shoe.

Caliban doesn't really want to lick Stefano's shoes in
this quote. He actually wants to kiss his feet. Obviously.

Riddle me this, riddle me that — do O.K. in the SAT...

You can get loads of marks in your SAT for talking about how Shakespeare uses comparisons.
If you can explain what it means when the characters are saying <u>weird</u> things, you'll be well away.

Why Characters Do Things

You can't predict exactly what they'll ask you in the exam — but some types of questions do come up a lot. Questions <u>about the characters</u> and why they do things are pretty common.

Write about *What They're Like*

> ### The Tempest
> Act 1 Scene 2 and Act 5 Scene 1
>
> **Is Prospero a good or a bad character?**
>
> Support your ideas by referring to the scenes.

For this question you need to go through the scene to find the bits that tell you <u>what Prospero wants</u> and <u>how he uses magic to achieve it</u>.

It helps if you go into the test with a pretty good idea about what the characters are like and what they do in the <u>rest</u> of the play.

Go through the *Scenes* and *Make Notes*

Prospero is the deposed Duke of Milan — he was deposed by his brother Antonio.

He seems to be a good man, but mischievous — he causes a storm to shipwreck his enemies in Act 1 Scene 2, but he doesn't really want to hurt them.

He forgives everyone who has hurt him in Act 5 Scene 1, but not before he's shouted at them all. He is obviously angry.

> *"I do forgive thee,*
> *Unnatural though thou art."*

Note down quotes. You'll need them later.

Watch when Characters talk *About Each Other*

Characters talk about each other — this gives you <u>useful information</u> about them. E.g. Here's what Caliban and Ariel say about Prospero in Act 3 Scene 2.

CALIBAN	As I told thee before, I am subject to a tyrant, A sorcerer, that by his cunning hath Cheated me of the island.
ARIEL	*(in* TRINCULO's *voice)* Thou liest.

You can find out a lot about the person <u>making</u> the comment as well as the person they're talking about. E.g. Caliban sounds pretty <u>bitter</u> when he talks about Prospero.

Why Characters Do Things

Remember, you're <u>only</u> expected to write about the <u>bits</u> of the play that they've <u>given you</u> to read. You <u>can</u> find an answer in there, if you look.

Get as Much as You Can from the Set Scenes

If you look at the scenes <u>thoroughly</u>, you can work out a lot about the characters.

> *Prospero openly admits in Act 1 Scene 2 that he didn't really pay attention to being a Duke — he was more interested in magic and learning. He allowed his brother Antonio to take power from under his nose.*

Remember who's Who

When writing about a character remember to talk about what their <u>position is in society</u> and <u>how they're related</u> to the other characters.

Remember to <u>quote</u> to show where your answer comes from.

> *Prospero is an outcast — he used to be a powerful Duke, but he was forced out by his brother Antonio and he now lives on a remote island. Apart from Prospero and his daughter, the only people on the island are the monster Caliban and spirits like Ariel. When he was a Duke he spent his time learning and studying magic, and now he's free to practise away from other distractions: "I thus neglecting worldly ends, all dedicated To closeness and the bettering of my mind."*
>
> *In Shakespeare's time a lot of people believed in magic and witchcraft — so although the story of the Tempest would still have been fantastic to audiences at the time, they would probably have believed it could really happen.*

Write about the Way that Characters Speak

Shakespeare gives the audience a <u>picture</u> of the characters by what they <u>say</u> and <u>how</u> they say it, <u>just</u> as much as by what they <u>do</u>.

> *Prospero speaks mainly in verse in the play. This shows that he is a noble character even though he is an outcast — he is still a wise man and a Duke, and ruler of his island. Characters in Shakespeare normally speak in verse if they are high born or noble characters and in prose if they are common or stupid people like Caliban the monster.*

Plays are full of vehicles pretending — 'car actors'...

<u>Read</u> the scenes carefully to find all the bits that tell you what the characters are <u>like</u>. Pay extra special attention to things they <u>say</u> about each other, and <u>how</u> they speak. Remember <u>who</u> the characters are — what their <u>relationships</u> are, and if they're the <u>king</u> or the <u>village idiot</u> or whatever.

How Characters Persuade

You might get a question about <u>how characters persuade</u> — especially for a play like <u>*Romeo and Juliet*</u> where there's a shedload of big speeches.

Here's a Classic *Persuading Question*

> **Romeo and Juliet**
> **Act 2 Scene 3**
> **Act 2 Scene 6**
>
> **How do Romeo and Juliet persuade those around them that their love is true?**
>
> Support your ideas with references to the following extracts.

1) To make your answer <u>really good</u> you'll have to make several points in your answer.

2) The <u>main things</u> you can write about for this question are the <u>language</u> Romeo and Juliet use, and what effect it has on all the <u>other characters</u> who appear in these two scenes.

Find some good examples of *Persuasive Language*

This is where you get to write about all the <u>tricks</u> of Shakespeare's <u>language</u> — see pages 41-46.

> Then plainly know my heart's dear love is set
> On the fair daughter of rich Capulet:
> As mine on hers, so hers is set on mine;
> And all combined, save what thou must combine
> By holy marriage.

Romeo is certain of his feelings for Juliet. He <u>convinces</u> Friar Lawrence of their love by <u>mixing</u> Juliet's feelings with descriptions of his own feelings.

> I pray thee, chide not. She whom I love now
> Doth grace for grace and love for love allow;
> The other did not so.

Romeo insists to Friar Lawrence that this love is <u>real</u> — his love of Rosaline was not.

Juliet <u>persuades</u> us of her love for Romeo through her use of <u>exaggeration</u>. She talks about how great her love is and how she can only just begin to put that love into words.

> But my true love is grown to such excess
> I cannot sum up sum of half my wealth.

> It cannot counterveil the exchange of joy
> That one short minute gives me in her sight.
> Do thou but close our hands with holy words,
> Then love-devouring death do what he dare,
> It is enough I may but call her mine.

Romeo convinces Friar Lawrence that marrying Juliet is the <u>only thing</u> that could bring him <u>happiness</u>.

How Characters Persuade

Write about What he's Trying to Do

Make it clear you understand what the character's <u>purpose</u> is. Make sure you mention <u>who</u> they're trying to persuade and <u>what</u> they want to persuade them of. Try to show you know how the extracts fit in with the rest of the play.

> *In Act 2 Scene 3, Friar Lawrence is surprised about Romeo's love for Juliet, reminding him that he used to love Rosaline and seemed to have forgotten her fairly quickly. Romeo responds by convincing the Friar of his genuine love for Juliet, and says that he wants the Friar to marry them.*

Don't fall into the trap of re-telling the story though. Just quickly outline his purpose before going on to the stuff below.

Say How he Tries to Persuade People

Next you need to say what <u>techniques</u> the character uses to try and get what they want. Use the <u>quotes</u> you've found and explain what they show you about the <u>methods of persuasion</u>:

Remember to explain the <u>effect</u> of the quotes you use.

> *Both Romeo and Juliet use romantic language and verse to convince people who know about their relationship that they are truly in love. Even the wise Friar Lawrence is convinced by Romeo that the relationship is a good idea.*
> *"But come, young waverer, come, go with me,*
> *In one respect I'll thy assistant be.*
> *For this alliance may so happy prove,*
> *To turn your households' rancour to pure love."*

Say How Successful he is

It's a good idea to comment on <u>how effective</u> the character's skills of persuasion are. One way to judge this is to look at how <u>other characters</u> respond.

> *Romeo and Juliet are so persuasive about their love that their guardians, Friar Lawrence and Nurse, are both convinced to help them marry. This is despite the wishes of the Capulet family for Juliet to marry Paris, and the feud between the Montagues and the Capulets.*

I love Romeo more than chocolate. And that's saying something.

Say <u>why</u> you think the character's attempts to persuade are <u>effective</u> or not.

A wallet on the scales — Purse-weighed...

This is **NOT THAT BAD**... there are <u>two things</u> you have to write about for persuasion questions — the <u>words</u> the character uses, and what the other characters <u>say and do</u> in reaction to their words.

Imagine You're Directing a Scene

These are 10 out of 10 for <u>fun</u>.*

*on a scale where 1 is having 10 teeth pulled, and 10 is having one tooth pulled

Think about the Audience

Directing a play means deciding <u>how</u> you want to <u>show</u> the <u>story</u> to the <u>audience</u>.

The <u>actors</u> have to play their parts so that the <u>audience</u> understand what's happening — and <u>feel</u> all the different <u>moods</u> that Shakespeare wanted them to feel when he wrote the play. That's what <u>you</u> have to <u>write about</u> in your <u>answer</u>.

The Audience Don't Have the Script in front of them

<u>You</u> have to <u>make</u> the audience understand what's happening — here are several ways to do this.

ANGRY SHOUTING

I'm ANGRY!

SHUT UP!

Ms. Angry

Make the actors <u>say</u> their lines in a way that <u>shows</u> the <u>feelings</u> of the character.

SWEET MUSIC

Hee hee, I'm so evil!

EVIL CLOTHES

Mr. Evil

Show the audience what a character is <u>like</u> by the <u>clothes</u> they wear.

Show the audience the <u>mood</u> of a scene by <u>lighting</u> and <u>sound</u>.

BLUE MOONLIGHT

I feel all romantic.

Mr. Romantic

You can write about all these things in your <u>answer</u>.

You have to Understand the Scene

Once again, <u>you</u> have to understand what's going on, because <u>you</u> have to say how you would <u>show</u> the <u>audience</u> what's going on.

That means you need to understand the <u>language</u>.

> The pow'rs, delaying, not forgetting, have
> Incensed the seas and shores, yea, all the creatures,
> Against your peace.

Ariel is telling Alonso and his followers that they're going to be punished in lots of weird and nasty ways for betraying Prospero — pretty scary stuff.

If you <u>don't understand</u> what a character's on about, it's very difficult to tell if they're sad, happy or angry.

Imagine You're Directing a Scene

Write about the Mood of the Scene

The mood of the scene is really important for this type of question. Some scenes are funny, some are scary, some are full of excitement and tension, some are spooky and some are romantic.

The mood of this scene is bleak and gloomy — Alonso is convinced his son has drowned, and says he just wants to find him and die with him.

O, it is monstrous, monstrous!
Methought the billows spoke, and told me of it,
The winds did sing it to me and the thunder,
That deep and dreadful organ-pipe, pronounced
The name of Prosper — it did bass my trespass.
Therefore my son i' th' ooze is bedded, and
I'll seek him deeper than e'er plummet sounded,
And with him there lie mudded.

The mood of the scene you get will be pretty clear. What you have to do in your answer is say which bits show the mood of the scene more than others.

You've Guessed it — Quote Lots

If you want an actor to speak a line in a particular way, then write that down. Give a quote.

I'll need all of these for loads of quotes.

When Caliban describes to Stephano how to kill Prospero, he could speak the line, "There thou mayst brain him", in a secretive whisper. This would show that he knows what he is saying could get him into trouble.

Quote a bit of the scene that really shows you what the mood of the scene is.

Mood — the sound cows made...

The trick to writing about directing a scene is to think about the audience's point of view. You have to show them what the mood of the scene is — with lights, sound, and the way things are said.

Writing About a Theme

Theme questions sound more tricky than they really are. They're generally just asking <u>how</u> the play puts across a particular <u>message</u> or <u>idea</u>.

Work Out What the Question is Asking

<u>Theme questions</u> are often worded like this:

> **Act 3 Scene 2, lines 41-154 and Act 5 Scene 1, lines 1-203**
> **How do these extracts show different attitudes to revenge in The Tempest?**
> *Support your ideas by referring to the scenes.*

<u>Don't panic</u> if the question seems complicated.

Read it carefully, and you'll realise it's actually pretty <u>simple</u>.

> You could rephrase this as:
> "Some of the characters in The Tempest want revenge on others. Why is this and how do they each try to get revenge?"

Theme Questions Aren't as Hard as They Look

1) Read through the scenes with the question in mind, and some points should pretty much <u>leap out</u> at you and give you the <u>basis for a good answer</u>. For example, for the question above, this quote from <u>Prospero</u> would be useful:

> Most cruelly
> Didst thou, Alonso, use me and my daughter.
> Thy brother was a furtherer in the act. —
> Thou art pinched for't now, Sebastian. — Flesh and blood,
> You, brother mine, that entertained ambition,
> Expelled remorse and nature, who, with Sebastian —
> Whose inward pinches therefore are most strong —
> Would here have killed your king, I do forgive thee,
> Unnatural though thou art.

Terribly sorry about the exile old bean...

2) Once you've found a good extract like this, just say <u>how it relates to the question</u>. Don't forget to stick in some good <u>quotes</u> to back up your points:

> Prospero is angry that he was betrayed by Alonso and Antonio but has put this aside and forgiven them, just as he has forgiven Sebastian for trying to murder Alonso on his island: "I do forgive thee, / Unnatural though thou art."

I don't like extracts — they remind me of dentists...

Questions about themes generally <u>tell you</u> an opinion, then ask you to <u>prove</u> that it's true. Which makes it <u>easy</u> really — no faffing about deciding what to argue, just find some good <u>evidence</u>.

Writing About a Theme

Here's a few more things you can do if you get a question about a <u>theme</u> or <u>issue</u>.

Each Play has Several Main Themes

If you do get a <u>theme question</u>, depending on the play, it's likely to be about one of these:

> **ROMEO AND JULIET**
> - forbidden love
> - family
> - honour
> - rivalry
> - innocence

> **THE TEMPEST**
> - fate and justice
> - magic
> - love
> - freedom
> - betrayal and forgiveness
> - slavery and service

Look for the Less Obvious Bits

1) There will usually be plenty of fairly <u>obvious points</u> you can use in your answer to a theme question.

2) But if you want to get really <u>great marks</u>, you'll need to go into a bit more <u>detail</u>. Try to write something that answers the question in a way that's <u>not</u> immediately obvious.

> *Maybe Prospero himself was only getting what he deserved when he lost his position as Duke of Milan. He admits that he was so obsessed with learning that he became guilty of "neglecting worldly ends". This seems to be what allowed Antonio's "falsehood" to develop — if Prospero had paid more attention to his duties, it is possible that Antonio would not have had the chance to abuse his trust.*

3) It's especially important that you give <u>evidence</u> for these kinds of points. The examiner might not have thought of this, so it's <u>vital</u> that you back it up with good <u>quotations</u>.

4) Don't go <u>over the top</u> trying to write blindingly original stuff — make sure you don't miss out the <u>clear-cut</u> points that'll give you easy marks. But if you can stick just <u>one or two</u> more unexpected, well-explained points into your plan, along with the easier stuff, they'll make your answer really <u>stand out</u>.

Exhibit A

> Make sure you stick to the question — it's easy to go off the point when you're trying to come up with a really original answer.

Where do topics go to have fun? A theme park...

You'll <u>never</u> get a question that asks you something unexpected, like "Explore how The Tempest suggests that life is all about eating squid". It'll always be a fairly <u>obvious</u> theme, so don't worry.

Huge Revision Question

Here's a lovely exam type <u>question</u> on *The Tempest*, all about extracts from <u>Act 3 Scene 2</u> and <u>Act 1 Scene 2</u>. It's the <u>length</u> of extract and the kind of <u>question</u> you'll get in the <u>exam</u>. Write out a good answer — make sure you practise all the <u>tricks</u> from this section.

> ## What do these two scenes tell us about the theme of loyalty in The Tempest?
>
> *Support your ideas with references to the following extracts.*

ACT 3 SCENE 2, lines 22 - 101

CALIBAN	How does thy honour? Let me lick thy shoe. I'll not serve him — he is not valiant.	
TRINCULO	Thou liest, most ignorant monster: I am in case to jostle a constable. Why, thou deboshed fish, thou, was there ever man a coward that hath drunk so much sack as I today? Wilt thou tell a monstrous lie, being but half a fish and half a monster?	25
CALIBAN	Lo, how he mocks me! Wilt thou let him, my lord?	
TRINCULO	'Lord' quoth he! That a monster should be such a natural!	
CALIBAN	Lo, lo again! Bite him to death, I prithee.	
STEPHANO	Trinculo, keep a good tongue in your head. If you prove a mutineer — the next tree! The poor monster's my subject, and he shall not suffer indignity.	30
CALIBAN	I thank my noble lord. Wilt thou be pleased to hearken once again to the suit I made to thee?	
STEPHANO	Marry will I — kneel and repeat it. I will stand, and so shall Trinculo.	

Enter ARIEL, *invisible*

CALIBAN	As I told thee before, I am subject to a tyrant, A sorcerer, that by his cunning hath Cheated me of the island.	35
ARIEL	*(in* TRINCULO's *voice)* Thou liest.	
CALIBAN	Thou liest, thou jesting monkey, thou. I would my valiant master would destroy thee. I do not lie.	40
STEPHANO	Trinculo, if you trouble him any more in's tale, by this hand, I will supplant some of your teeth.	
TRINCULO	Why, I said nothing.	
STEPHANO	Mum, then, and no more. Proceed.	45
CALIBAN	I say, by sorcery he got this isle — From me he got it. If thy greatness will Revenge it on him — for I know thou dar'st, But this thing dare not —	
STEPHANO	That's most certain.	50

Huge Revision Question

CALIBAN   Thou shalt be lord of it, and I'll serve thee.
STEPHANO How now shall this be compassed? Canst thou bring me to the party?
CALIBAN   Yea, yea, my lord, I'll yield him thee asleep,
                  Where thou mayst knock a nail into his head.

ARIEL   *(in* TRINCULO's *voice)* Thou liest — thou canst not.   55

CALIBAN   What a pied ninny's this! Thou scurvy patch!
                  I do beseech thy greatness, give him blows,
                  And take his bottle from him. When that's gone
                  He shall drink nought but brine, for I'll not show him
                  Where the quick freshes are.   60
STEPHANO Trinculo, run into no further danger. Interrupt the monster
                  one word further and, by this hand, I'll turn my mercy out
                  o' doors, and make a stockfish of thee.
TRINCULO Why, what did I? I did nothing. I'll go farther off.
STEPHANO Didst thou not say he lied?   65

ARIEL   *(in* TRINCULO's *voice)* Thou liest.

STEPHANO Do I so? Take thou that. *(beats Trinculo)* As you like this,
                  give me the lie another time.
TRINCULO I did not give the lie. Out o' your wits and hearing too? A pox o' your bottle! This
                  can sack and drinking do. A murrain on your monster, and the devil take your   70
                  fingers!
CALIBAN   Ha, ha, ha!
STEPHANO Now, forward with your tale. *(to* TRINCULO*)* Prithee stand further off.
CALIBAN   Beat him enough — after a little time,
                  I'll beat him too.   75
STEPHANO Stand farther. Come, proceed.
CALIBAN   Why, as I told thee, 'tis a custom with him
                  I' th' afternoon to sleep. There thou mayst brain him,
                  Having first seized his books, or with a log
                  Batter his skull, or paunch him with a stake,   80
                  Or cut his wezand with thy knife. Remember
                  First to possess his books, for without them
                  He's but a sot, as I am, nor hath not
                  One spirit to command. They all do hate him
                  As rootedly as I. Burn but his books.   85
                  He has brave utensils — for so he calls them —
                  Which, when he has a house, he'll deck withal.
                  And that most deeply to consider is
                  The beauty of his daughter — he himself
                  Calls her a nonpareil. I never saw a woman   90
                  But only Sycorax my dam and she,
                  But she as far surpasseth Sycorax
                  As great'st does least.

Huge Revision Question

STEPHANO	Is it so brave a lass?
CALIBAN	Ay, lord. She will become thy bed, I warrant,
	And bring thee forth brave brood. 95
STEPHANO	Monster, I will kill this man. His daughter and I will be King and Queen — save our Graces! — and Trinculo and thyself shall be viceroys. Dost thou like the plot, Trinculo?
TRINCULO	Excellent.
STEPHANO	Give me thy hand — I am sorry I beat thee, but while thou liv'st, keep a 100 good tongue in thy head.

ACT 1 SCENE 2, lines 89 - 119

PROSPERO   I pray thee, mark me.
I thus neglecting worldly ends, all dedicated   90
To closeness and the bettering of my mind
With that which, but by being so retired,
O'er-prized all popular rate, in my false brother
Awaked an evil nature, and my trust,
Like a good parent, did beget of him   95
A falsehood, in its contrary as great
As my trust was, which had indeed no limit,
A confidence sans bound. He being thus lorded,
Not only with what my revenue yielded,
But what my power might else exact, like one   100
Who having into truth, by telling of it,
Made such a sinner of his memory,
To credit his own lie, he did believe
He was indeed the Duke, out o' th' substitution,
And executing th' outward face of royalty   105
With all prerogative. Hence his ambition growing —
Dost thou hear?

MIRANDA   Your tale, sir, would cure deafness.
PROSPERO
To have no screen between this part he played
And him he played it for, he needs will be
Absolute Milan. Me, poor man, my library   110
Was dukedom large enough. Of temporal royalties
He thinks me now incapable, confederates —
So dry he was for sway — wi' th' King of Naples,
To give him annual tribute, do him homage,
Subject his coronet to his crown, and bend   115
The dukedom, yet unbowed — alas, poor Milan! —
To most ignoble stooping.

MIRANDA   O the heavens!
PROSPERO
Mark his condition, and th' event, then tell me
If this might be a brother.

What You Have to Do

Writing... a <u>tough nut</u> to crack. Unless you're a squirrel that is.

You Have to do *Two Writing Questions*

There are <u>two</u> parts to the Writing Paper:

1)   <u>The Long Writing Question</u>: you have to read a short bit of writing which sets the scene, then write something connected with that bit of writing.

Read the question all the way <u>through</u>...

2)   <u>The Short Writing Question</u>: there's a short bit of writing which sets the scene, then a task that's based on it.

IN THE SAT: Don't <u>rush</u> into doing the writing. Read the <u>questions</u> carefully before you start.

Show Off *these* Five *things in* Your Writing

The <u>examiners</u> want to see how good you are at the <u>nuts and bolts of writing</u>. Here's what they're looking for:

One... two... three... er... six?

1) <u>GOOD SPELLING</u>
So always <u>check</u> over what you've written for mistakes.

2) <u>PROPER SENTENCES</u>
i.e. sentences with <u>full punctuation</u>, that <u>make sense</u>.

3) <u>WELL-ORGANISED WRITING</u>
That means writing in <u>paragraphs</u>, having an <u>introduction</u> and a clear <u>ending</u>, and a sensible <u>order</u> to all the points you make in between.

4) <u>THE RIGHT STYLE</u>
e.g. If you're asked for a magazine article use <u>words</u> and <u>phrases</u> that make your writing <u>sound like</u> a magazine article.

5) <u>SIGNS YOU'VE THOUGHT ABOUT THE READER</u>
If it's a piece for <u>young kids</u> keep it <u>simple</u> so they can understand. If it's for your gran don't use the kind of language you'd use to your friends at school. Make sure it's <u>interesting</u> enough to keep your reader from nodding off too.

Insect writing exams — ants-er the question...

<u>Don't panic</u> when you're doing writing questions. Take a deep breath, read through the whole thing <u>carefully</u>, and remember what they're looking for — good writing not amazing ideas.

The Long Writing Question

The two writing questions aren't <u>wildly</u> different. But they're not exactly the same either — <u>learn the difference</u> now so you don't make any unfortunate boobs on the day.

The Long Writing Question Looks Like This...

There's quite <u>a lot</u> to read for these tasks. Read through it all <u>carefully</u> a couple of times, so you know <u>exactly</u> what it is they want you to do.

This bit of writing sets the scene. Read it <u>carefully</u>.

Your whiskers tickle

This is an extract from the paper the *Daily Hail*.

The Daily Hail

Fur Will Fly at No.10

The Editor writes:
What's going on at 10 Downing Street? First we learn that Humphrey the cat's not allowed in the offices. Now we learn he's been confined to the kitchen. And there's <u>no cat flap</u>. What kind of life is this for a cat that's served the nation for nine and a half years? I'm disgusted, Prime Minister, and I believe the British public is disgusted too.

As a reader of the "Daily Hail", write a letter to the Prime Minister, agreeing or disagreeing with the article.

This is what you've actually got to <u>do</u>.

1) <u>Pretend</u> you're someone who reads the "Daily Hail".

2) <u>Write a letter</u> to the <u>Prime Minister</u>.
   Use the right <u>language</u>, and <u>lay it out</u> like a proper letter.

3) <u>Agree</u> with the article... OR... <u>disagree</u> with the article.

What You Need to Know

1) You should spend <u>45 minutes</u> in total on this question. Spend <u>15 minutes</u> <u>planning</u>. Spend <u>25 minutes writing</u>. Leave about <u>5 minutes</u> at the end to check over what you've written.

2) It's called the 'long' writing question, but you <u>don't</u> have to write pages and pages. A bit over <u>300 words</u> should do it.

Don't get carried away

Deciding What to Say

You'll be able to use <u>ideas from the article</u> to work out what you're going to say.

For this question you could pick out all the points the editor makes, then agree or disagree with each point.

The Short Writing Question

Did I hear a sigh of <u>boredom</u> as you turned to this page... Just a little one... I'm sure I did...
These may not be the most interesting pages in the book, but they sure as ham are <u>useful</u>.

The Short Writing Question Looks Like This...

It starts with a short <u>introduction</u> to the topic.

> Some teachers at your school are worried that pupils are under too much pressure to achieve high grades.
>
> *The following is printed in your school newspaper:*

Then there's a bit <u>setting the scene</u> for the piece you've got to write.

> We want to know what <u>you</u> think about pressure at school.
>
> Tell us whether you find school stressful or not. Do you feel under pressure from teachers, in exams, or on the sports field?
>
> Do your parents put you under pressure to do well? If so, what effect is all this stress having on you?

You'll get a few <u>hints</u> about what to write about. These hints are really helpful — <u>use them</u>.

Write the article for the school newspaper.

If they say article they mean <u>article</u>. Don't go writing a letter or a speech.

What You Need to Know

1) You get <u>20 marks</u> for this task.
2) Spend about <u>10 minutes planning</u> and <u>20</u> writing.
3) You need to write about <u>200 words</u> for this one.
   Keep your writing <u>organised</u> and <u>stick to the point</u>.
   You haven't got <u>time</u> to write a long waffly essay.

Skip the waffle. Get straight to the point.

Use the Hints You're Given

- Time's <u>short</u>.
- They give marks for <u>how well you write</u>, not for brilliant ideas.
- Using the <u>hints</u> in the question is the <u>quickest</u> way to get started.

A Short Writing Task...

The two writing questions are a bit different, so you have to tackle them in different ways.
Not that different though. Not as different as a <u>cockroach</u> and the Mona Lisa.

Work Out What To Say

Once you've read the question, work out <u>what</u> you're going to say to answer it. That means making a <u>plan</u>.

Decide What To Say Before You Start

You've got to have a <u>good think</u> about what you're going to write about <u>before</u> you start. You don't need to know exactly what you're going to write, but you need to have a rough idea.

> Good writing <u>makes a point</u>. It doesn't just ramble on about nothing.

Whether you're writing a story, a description, a letter or an opinion piece, make sure you've got <u>enough ideas</u> to keep you writing till your time's up — without having to waffle.

Jot Down your Points into a Rough Plan

It's a good idea to jot down a <u>plan</u> of the points you want to make <u>before</u> you start writing. That way you don't get to the end and realise you've <u>forgotten</u> something.

> Q. Write an article for a newspaper about an issue that's important to you. Explain why you think the issue is important.

(1) A plan doesn't have to be in proper sentences. It's just a <u>reminder</u> for you to use.

(2) <u>Start</u> with what you think is the <u>most important</u> point. This grabs your reader's attention.

(3) Try to <u>link</u> your points together. You can link smoothly from meat to treatment of animals.

> PLAN: *Modern farming methods.*
>
> *Reducing quality of soil — less food can be grown — soon we won't have enough to eat.*
>
> *Risks to human health — pesticides — antibiotics in meat.*
>
> *Animals treated badly — profits more important than welfare.*
>
> *What we can do — buy organic.*

(4) Work out how you're going to <u>end</u> your piece. This is a positive ending — it says what we can do.

No rambling — so no walking boots needed...

Obviously, writing that <u>rambles on</u> without getting anywhere <u>isn't</u> going to get the best <u>marks</u>. Work out roughly what you're going to say <u>before</u> you start writing. It helps to jot down a <u>plan</u>. All this needs to be second nature by the time you get to the Exam, so <u>get learning</u>.

Stories Need Planning Too

It's not only questions which ask for your opinion that need <u>planning</u>. You should <u>also</u> make a plan if you're doing a <u>story</u> question. Even <u>description</u> pieces will be better with a plan.

Plan _What Will_ Happen _In Your Story_

It's tempting just to start by writing "once upon a time..." and hope that you'll be able to make up what happens in your story <u>as you go along</u>. But that's a <u>really bad</u> idea.

<u>Before</u> you start to write your story, you should have a good idea of how it's going to <u>end</u>, and what's going to happen in the <u>middle</u>. Otherwise you'll get in all sorts of <u>problems</u>.

Q. Write about an exciting journey you have made.
It can be real or imaginary.

> PLAN: _Going on holiday on a plane._
>
> _Everyone except me got very ill from the food._
>
> _Went to the cockpit — pilot was unconscious._
>
> _I talked to air traffic control over the pilot's radio and they told me what to do._
>
> _I landed the plane safely._
>
> _Everyone went to hospital — they were all fine._

This plan is like a <u>summary</u> of the story you're going to write.

When you write the <u>story</u>, you could have two or three paragraphs about <u>each</u> of these points.

You've <u>planned</u> how it's going to <u>end</u>, so you always know what you're aiming towards.

Even _Description_ Pieces Need A Plan

When you're <u>describing</u> something, there isn't a beginning, a middle and an end like in a story. But you <u>still</u> need to know what kind of things you're going to say.

Quiet? Eh?

Q. Describe your favourite place.

PLAN: _Down by the river — peaceful and pretty — lots of grass — friends — go swimming in summer — ice skating in winter — friendly horse in nearby field — lots of trees — lovely colours in autumn — wild flowers in spring._

It might not look like much, but notes like this can <u>really help</u> you. You're not going to get <u>stuck</u> and <u>panic</u> because you run out of ideas for things to write.

Stories need a quiche? — I said plan, not FLAN...

Whatever it is you've got to write, having a <u>plan</u> can really help you. If you start writing <u>without</u> a plan, you're likely to <u>run out</u> of ideas or find you're waffling on about nothing at all.

Use The Right Style

Using the right writing <u>style</u> to write your answer is very important. You'll <u>lose</u> marks if you choose the <u>wrong</u> style, or if you <u>change</u> styles halfway through your answer.

Write in the Right Style to Fit the Question

Each question needs you to write in a certain <u>style</u>. Look at what the question is <u>telling</u> you to do, and use your common sense to decide what style to write in.

If you're asked to write a travel brochure, use loads of <u>fancy phrases</u> — like this.

Golden sandy beaches and gently lapping waves await you on the island of Noonos. Soak up the sun and forget your worldly cares with a refreshing swim in the warm, crystal-clear sea...

The faulty pelican crossing has caused ten accidents. Do you want to run that risk? We must take action now before someone else is injured — or even killed. Write to your local councillor at once.

If the question tells you to write a speech, be <u>snappy</u>, <u>punchy</u> and <u>direct</u> — like this.

If the question tells you to write a <u>horror</u> story, use words that give a feeling of <u>fear</u> and <u>suspense</u> — like this.

Slowly, the thick oak door creaked open. Emma quaked with fear. The clock ticked loudly. Then — bang! The ear-piercing crack of a gunshot filled the room. Emma screamed.

Use Fancy Words if you Need them

Some writing styles tend to involve lots of fancy words.
Don't be afraid to use them — but only if you're <u>sure</u> you know what they <u>mean</u>.

The important thing is to show you <u>know</u> what kind of style you're supposed to be using.
You'll get marks for <u>trying</u> — even if the spelling of the long words is a bit wonky.

Like a Makeover show — it's a Style Challenge...

It's very important that you get the <u>style</u> right — or at least that you <u>show</u> you <u>understand</u> what sort of style you should be using. Make sure that's in your mind when you answer the question.

Writing Letters

It's especially important to get your writing style right when you have to write a <u>letter</u>.
If you're asked to write a letter, sort out whether it's <u>formal</u> or <u>informal</u>. Here's how...

Formal Letters need Formal Language

<u>Formal</u> letters are to people you <u>don't know</u> very well. They are things like a letter of
<u>complaint</u>, a letter <u>requesting information</u>, or a letter from your <u>headteacher</u> to your <u>parent</u>.

Q. Write a letter to a supermarket manager complaining about poor quality food you bought at their store.

Dear Sir/Madam,

I wish to inform you that I contracted food poisoning from a fish finger bought at your store. I purchased the item on Saturday March 14th and consumed it that night. It made me severely ill for several days.

Yours faithfully,

Osborn Outhouse (Mr.)

> The letter uses <u>long words</u> and the tone is very <u>formal</u>.

> If you start a formal letter "Dear <u>Sir/Madam</u>," always end with "Yours <u>faithfully</u>". If you know the <u>name</u> of the person you're writing to, use "Yours <u>sincerely</u>".

(In an <u>exam</u> these letters would be much <u>longer</u>.)

Informal Letters are Chatty

Letters to your <u>friends</u> are <u>informal</u>. You know your friends <u>well</u> — so you don't need to use
formal language with them. Write in a <u>chatty</u> style, like you'd use if you were <u>talking</u> to them.

Q. Write a letter to a friend about something that happened to you recently.

> The language is very <u>chatty</u> and <u>informal</u>. You wouldn't write this way to a stranger.

Dear Fred,

I've been feeling rotten these last few days. I ate a dodgy fish finger from the store. It whistled right through my system, I can tell you. I was throwing up all night. I'd steer well clear of them if I were you, mate.

See you soon,

Ossie

> <u>Don't</u> end informal letters with "Yours faithfully" or "Yours sincerely". Write something like "<u>love</u>" or "<u>best wishes</u>" instead.

> There's no need to give your <u>full</u> name — your friends know who you are.

A laid-back salad — informal lettuce...

If the question asks you to write a <u>letter</u>, stop and think about <u>who</u> the letter is to. <u>Don't</u> be
<u>chatty</u> in a letter to someone you <u>don't know</u>, and don't be <u>formal</u> in a letter to a <u>friend</u>.

Revision Summary Questions

As if the reading part of your SATs wasn't enough, you've got to learn all this stuff about writing as well. Oh well — it has to be done. You wouldn't think there were so many tricks to doing something as simple as writing, but trust me — making sure you know all the stuff in this section will make a huge difference to the mark you get. Don't be a schmuck and think you can wing it. Go over this section till you can answer every last one of these questions.

1) How many writing questions do you have to do for the SAT?

2) What five things should you do as well as you can on the writing tasks?

3) What does it mean when the task says "you could write about..."?

4) Why are story questions often harder to do than you might think?

5) For the short question, should you:
   a) use the hints you're given
   b) ignore the hints — they're just there to catch you out

6) When should you decide what you should say in your answer?
   a) before you start writing it, in a plan.
   b) as you go along.
   c) over a cup of tea at home afterwards.

7) What type of answer *don't* you need a plan for?
   a) Stories,
         b) Description pieces,
               c) Opinion questions,
                     d) Ones you want to do badly on.

8) When you're writing about your opinions, when should you use your strongest point?

9) What should you make sure the style you write in matches?

10) How do you decide whether a letter is supposed to be formal or informal?

11) How do you end a formal letter when you know the name of the person you're writing to? And when you don't know their name?

12) In which type of letter should you use chatty language?

13) List a few ways you could end an informal letter.

That's not *quite* what I meant...

Paragraphs

Paragraphs are a <u>big hassle</u>, but you get <u>more marks</u> for using them. Your writing's loads clearer when you use paragraphs — you need to know how to use 'em properly.

Always Use Paragraphs

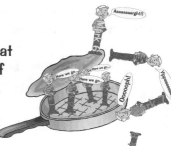

Yes, you actually <u>get marks</u> for writing in paragraphs. The flip side is that you <u>lose marks</u> if you don't. It's not enough to use paragraphs <u>some</u> of the time — you need to use them <u>all</u> the time — in <u>stories</u> and <u>essays</u>.

Paragraphs Make Things Clear

Crystal clear?

A paragraph is a group of sentences. These sentences talk about the same thing, or follow on from each other.

Every new paragraph must have a space between the margin and the first word.
Leave another space every time you start a new paragraph. This shows you're writing about something different.

Leave a little gap before the first word.

When you finish the last line of the paragraph, just stop.

Start a New Paragraph for Each Point in an Essay

Paragraphs help make your essay <u>clearer</u>.
A new paragraph shows that you're writing about <u>something new</u>.

This is a new point, so start a new paragraph.

Stick to the point.

The idea that school uniforms hide the difference between rich and poor is a fantasy. Everyone can tell whose uniform came from a discount store and whose came from a designer shop.
Supporters of school uniform say that they don't want to turn school into a "fashion parade". In fact, this is exactly what they are doing when they point out the tiny ways in which a skirt or jumper doesn't quite fit the rules.

Applying to University — fill in a Uni-form...

Paragraphs — love 'em or hate 'em, you've got to use them. Start a <u>new paragraph</u> each and every time you start a new sentence with a brand <u>new</u> idea, or <u>angle</u>, or <u>argument</u>. Make it clear as day to everyone — especially the examiners — that you have a shiny new point to make.

Using Paragraphs

You need to know when to start a new paragraph — you can't guess. I know it's tough, but you'll have to learn the rules. Here's a nice golden rule to start with...

Here's the Golden Rule for Paragraphs

Start a new paragraph every time something changes.

When you Talk about a New Person

This paragraph is about Tanya.

I can't believe what a mess you've made.

> Tanya looked at the scene in despair. She couldn't believe that eight soldiers could make such a mess. She sighed and started to pick up the biscuits and crisps.
>
> A friendly face popped round the door. It was Brian. He watched Tanya grovelling around in the mess for a second or two before he spoke up.

This paragraph is about Brian.

When Someone New Speaks

The same person is speaking here, so you don't need a new paragraph.

Someone new is speaking, so you need a new paragraph.

> "Please don't do that on your own, Tanya," said Brian. "Come on, I'll help you clear up," he offered.
> "Thanks, Brian, you're a star," replied Tanya appreciatively. "Where's everyone else? I thought there were five volunteers to clear up."
> "They're all dancing over there," he explained.

I'll help you clear up.

You're a star...

Using Paragraphs

Paragraphs are great. But there's no point in knowing that if you don't know when to use them. Here are <u>two more</u> times when you need to start a new paragraph.

A New Paragraph for a New Place...

> The shopping mall was utterly deserted. The uniformed security guards scratched their heads. What were they supposed to do now there was no-one to watch?
>
> Outside Bernie's gourmet chip shop in the High Street it was a rather different story. The crowd was three deep around the shop, all pushing and shoving to get to the door. "Give us battered rat!" they clamoured. "Give us rat on a stick!".

No rats were harmed in the making of this page.

The story has moved to the chip shop, so this is a new paragraph.

...or for a Different Time

This is talking about later that day.

This is talking about a long time afterwards.

> At last it was over. The voice called out again, "Are you alright?" I barely had the strength to answer. Relief flooded through me in a warm, drowsy wave. Soon I would be out of the cave and home.
>
> An hour later I was sitting in the coastguard's van, drinking hot tea from a flask. I could hear people talking all around me, but I couldn't really understand what they were saying. It was all a bit too much for me to take in. All I knew was that I was safe and everything was going to be alright.
>
> I don't think about my ordeal that much. When I look back, it seems like something that happened to somebody else. I can't believe that I could have been so reckless.

A herby fish dish — thyme and plaice...

Every time you <u>change time</u> or <u>place</u> in a <u>story</u>, a <u>letter</u> or an <u>essay</u> you have to use a new <u>paragraph</u>. No ifs, no buts — it's as simple as that. It's got to be <u>second nature</u> in the Exam.

Revision Summary Questions

Well, here we are at the end of another section, and what do you know, it's time for a set of revision summary questions. Remember, the point of these little jokers is to make sure that you've learnt something from the last three pages. Go through them, and don't you dare move on to the next section until you've got them all right. Ooh, I can be tough when I want to be...

1) What is a paragraph?

2) Do paragraphs make your writing a) clearer b) really complicated?

3) What should you do at the start of a paragraph?

4) What should you do at the end of the last line in a paragraph?

5) Do paragraphs make: a) not the blindest bit of difference to your mark

   b) a major difference to your mark   c) a nice accompaniment to steak and chips?

6) What is the golden rule for starting a new paragraph?

7) What's the rule when you're writing about new people?

8) What's the rule for when people are speaking?

9) Do you need to start a new paragraph when the same person carries on speaking?

10) What's the rule for changes of place?

11) What's the rule for changes of time? (you should be spotting some kind of pattern here...)

12) The following piece is really confusing. Turn it into a nice clear bit of writing by rewriting it with proper paragraphs:

The biggest challenge facing junior league football today is the sheer number of red and yellow cards issued by referees. There is no doubt that standards of discipline have fallen sharply. Last year, 85 yellow cards and 14 red cards were issued in the first six weeks of the season. Already this year 136 yellow cards and 26 red cards have been issued. 4 players are facing a four-match ban. Hector Dalrymple, chairman of the UK federation of under-16 Football clubs, said last week that the situation was "reaching crisis point". Some, like Julian Fortescue of Edenhall School, disagree.

13) Write three paragraphs of a story, using the rules in this section.

14) Write a short essay about your school, using the rules in this section.

There's more than one way to divide writing into bite size chunks...

Basic Punctuation

This stuff is about as basic as it gets. People do get it wrong though — when they're <u>rushing</u> and not <u>thinking</u>. Learn it really well, and you won't even <u>need</u> to think about it.

Don't Lose Marks for Simple Stuff

Right, now this is stuff that you already know, but it doesn't hurt to go over it again.

Every sentence starts with a <u>capital letter</u>, and ends with a <u>full stop</u>.

This is the bit you have to think about more carefully.

The names of <u>people</u>, <u>places</u>, <u>organisations</u>, <u>days of the week</u> and <u>months of the year</u> ALL NEED CAPITAL LETTERS.

You haven't seen Ben since Monday.

Capital letter   Capital letter   Full stop

My aunt works in the marketing department of Ace Products.

Capital letter   Capital letters   Full stop

We're going on holiday to Greece in August.

Capital letter   Capital letter   Capital letter   Full stop

Questions need Question marks

If a sentence is a question it's got to have a question mark. Don't forget.

Boris, can you see Mrs Marple?

Only Use One Exclamation Mark

It was absolutely amazing! I couldn't believe I was really meeting Russian pop sensations, Steppes!!!!

NO!

This makes your writing look silly, and you'll lose marks for it.

Getting this wrong — it's a capital crime...

OK, this is something that's <u>so basic</u> you'd only get it wrong if you weren't <u>awake</u>. What you have to do is make sure you <u>can</u> do it <u>in your sleep</u> — that way you won't make <u>daft mistakes</u>.

Sentences

Everything you write has to be in proper sentences, or you're just throwing away marks.

Every Sentence makes a Clear Point

A sentence that doesn't make sense isn't much use to anyone.

The Golden Rule
Every sentence must make sense on its own.

Don't let your Sentences Run on and on

We've run on too long...

Don't let your sentences all run together into a huge long mess.

> *The doorbell rang it was Theo he asked if I wanted a game of five-a-side.*

This type of long messy sentence will lose you marks.

> *The doorbell rang. It was Theo. He asked if I wanted a game of five-a-side.*

This sentence makes one point, and it's clear.

These sentences are short, but they're proper sentences.

A Sentence has to have a Verb

For a sentence to make sense, it has to be about something. It can only be about something happening if it's got a verb. Remember, verbs are doing and being words.

"Cost" is the verb.

> *Barry bought a champion racing ram. It cost £2.50.*

This is about him buying the ram.

This is about the ram costing £2.50.

Move it!

> *Barry bought a champion racing ram. For £2.50.*

You can't do this. There's no verb, so this isn't a sentence.

A see-through pin — that's a clear point...

Working out when a sentence should end takes a little bit of thought. If you're rushing like crazy in the Exam, you'll forget about it. Keep your sentences manageable — don't let them turn into huge great gargantuan monsters. Remember this, too — no verb, no sentence.

Commas

Commas are horrible annoying little things. You're definitely going to <u>need</u> them in your writing Exam, so make sure you know how to <u>use</u> them.

Use Commas to Break up Sentences

If a sentence has <u>more</u> than one point, a comma keeps the points <u>separate</u>. Commas keep the items in <u>lists</u> separate, too.

I asked him to shut up, but he kept on yelling.

The comma keeps these two bits <u>separate</u>.

Commas add Extra bits to Sentences

After the match, we all went to Kathy's house for tea and toast.

Annie and Bert, who live next door, have built a bomb shelter.

The extra bit's in the middle of this sentence. The commas go around it like little <u>brackets</u>.

When you start a sentence with words like "<u>Oh</u>", "<u>Right</u>" or "<u>Well</u>", you need a <u>comma</u> to separate it from the rest of the sentence.

Now then, I think you need to lose that hat.

Well, I suppose you might just get away with it.

Don't Stick them in All Over the place

The Mayor, Mrs Thribblewort, and the Treasurer, Mr Branchwood, said today, that the community centre would open on the 14th of September.

Don't just chuck me in!

This comma's actually <u>wrong</u> — "said today" and "that the community centre..." go together — they're part of the <u>same</u> bit of info.

You should <u>only</u> put commas in when you want to <u>break</u> a sentence up into <u>two bits</u> or when you want to stick in a bit of <u>extra</u> information. <u>Randomly</u> throwing in a bunch of commas <u>isn't</u> going to work.

Blend in — be a comma chameleon...

Commas keep things <u>apart</u> in sentences. Make sure you use them to bracket off extra bits of information, but don't chuck them around willy-nilly. <u>Learn</u> the <u>right way</u> to use them.

Apostrophes

Lots of people mess this up — so get it learned. Make sure you know it <u>so</u> well that you'll <u>NEVER</u> forget it. When you've read it, cover the page and scribble down what's on it, then <u>check</u> you've got it right.

Use *Apostrophes* *to show who* *Owns* *something*

Mine, all mine!

Kulvinder's goldfish have all died.

When it's a group of people ending in s, add an <u>apostrophe</u>, but no <u>s</u>.

I washed the judges' wigs in soy sauce.

'Men', 'women' and 'children' follow the normal rule.

The women's race was cancelled.

Apostrophes are used in *short forms* *of words*

You need apostrophes for making <u>short</u> forms of words — like <u>we're</u> instead of <u>we are</u>.

I'm	he's	who's
I'd	won't	doesn't
I've	can't	here's
we'll	they're	we're

All of these need <u>apostrophes</u>. <u>Learn</u> them. Don't let the <u>easy</u> marks slip away.

Its and It's are Two Different Words

Getting <u>it's</u> and <u>its</u> mixed up is a mistake that people make all the time. They <u>are</u> confusing and they cause <u>more hassle</u> than anything else in English spelling. Get them <u>sorted out</u>.

The whale flipped <u>its</u> tail.

Its = <u>belonging</u> to it.

You <u>don't</u> use an apostrophe with <u>his</u> or <u>hers</u>, so <u>don't</u> use one with <u>its</u>.

It's thrown them into the air.

This is short for '<u>it has</u>'.

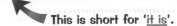

It's a long way down, captain.

This is short for '<u>it is</u>'.

An award for postmen — a post trophy...

Remember to put in your <u>apostrophes</u> or you can wave goodbye to a lot of marks. You really do have to <u>learn</u> the stuff about <u>its</u> and <u>it's</u>. Every time you use one of them, <u>think</u> about it.

Speech Marks

Speech marks do just what the name says — they show when someone's speaking.
All you've got to to do is use them in all the right places. You've guessed it — learn this page...

Speech Marks show when Someone is Speaking

Speech marks go at the start of the speech...

... and speech marks go at the end of the speech.

"These aren't my shoes," said Kevin.

You need speech marks because these are the words that Kevin said.

I won't ask Mary said.

This isn't clear without the speech marks...

...for a second, it looks like someone's saying that they won't ask Mary.

"I won't ask," Mary said.

You can see what's being said here.

When to Use Speech Marks

Be careful. You don't need speech marks if there's no one talking in your sentence.
Remember, though, every time someone actually speaks in a sentence, put speech marks.

NO SPEECH MARKS HERE

Tony said that he would lend Kevin a pair of trainers.

You don't need speech marks here.
No one's actually speaking.

SPEECH MARKS

Tony said, "I'll lend you a pair of trainers."

Look out! Someone is speaking in this sentence.
You need speech marks here, and don't you forget it.

Remember to always use speech marks when you quote from a piece of writing.
See Section 3 for stuff about quoting.

Speech Marks

Other bits of punctuation have to fit in with speech marks, too. Learn these two rules.

Start with a Capital Letter

"Don't leave the cage door open," warned Sally.

It starts with a capital letter.

Harry said, "Don't worry, I won't."

The spoken bit always starts with a capital letter, even if it isn't at the beginning of the sentence.

End with a Full Stop, a Comma or a Question Mark

Ruby said, "I knew you shouldn't have trusted Harry."

The sentence is finished, so you need a full stop.

"He doesn't know if he's coming or going," she declared.

The speech has finished but the sentence hasn't. You need a comma here, not a full stop.

"Had the bear been fed before it escaped?" asked Jill.

This is a question, so here's a question mark. Ace...

Don't forget — a question needs a question mark.

Speech marks — 10 out of 10 for a good 'un...

Don't EVER forget to put speech marks around something that a person's actually saying. The page on punctuation in speech marks is a bit harder, so make sure you learn the rules.

Revision Summary Questions

*You have to pay attention to all the little bitty things like full stops and apostrophes.
It's a major pain, but you've got to learn all this boring punctuation. It's no good being
sort of vaguely aware of it. You have to know it back to front and inside out so that
you don't make mistakes even when you're in a hurry. You don't want to be losing
marks for getting the easy bits wrong. The only way to make sure you know it all is to
go over these questions until you get every single one right.*

1) What's wrong with this sentence?
   I've got tickets to see the raiders play the vikings on saturday.

2) What should you never do with exclamation marks?

3) What's the Golden Rule of Sentences?

4) Rewrite this as three proper sentences:
   *I had to find out where the sound was coming from, as I walked closer I got more
   and more nervous, I wanted to scream, but nothing came out of my mouth.*

5) Why isn't this a sentence? *Under a palm tree with a cool drink.* What's missing?

6) Are these proper sentences? If not, write a proper sentence instead:
   a) I enjoyed my holiday. b) The sea was warm. c) To the beach.

7) Put a comma in the right place to show there are two clear points here:
   Before I could warn him the General sat firmly down on the broken chair.

8) Put commas in the right places to show which is the extra information: *The masked
   mathematician her hair streaming out behind her hurtled towards the long division sum.*

9) My mate Flat Head doesn't bother learning punctuation.
   She just scatters commas through her writing and hopes.
   Will she: *a)* get most of them right? *b)* make a bit of a mess of it?

10) What two things do apostrophes do?

11) What's the difference between its and it's?

12) Rewrite this properly: *This food mixer is brilliant. It's slicing attachment chops vegetables
    really quickly. Its got a separate liquidiser for soups and milk shakes.*

13) Put speech marks into these sentence:
    Earth has nothing better than a nice cosy armchair murmured Harry.

14) What's wrong with this sentence?
    The masked mathematician said "next week I can show you how the equation was solved"

Use Different Words

Writing 'properly' isn't enough — your writing has to be <u>interesting</u> too. A good way to start making your writing more interesting is to make sure you use lots of <u>different words</u>.

Use Different Words For The Same Thing

English has lots of words that mean the <u>same thing</u> as other words. That sounds a bit pointless. But it's actually <u>really handy</u>. Writing is very <u>dull</u> if it uses the same words all the time.

Have a look at these two pieces of writing and you'll see what I mean.

DULL

I went to a nice Indian restaurant last night. The waiters were nice to us and the walls were painted in a nice shade of red. I had an onion bhaji to start with and it was really nice. Then I had a nice curry. After the meal the waiters brought us mints, which was nice of them.

It may be 'correctly' written and make perfect sense, but it's dead <u>boring</u> — the word '<u>nice</u>' is in it again and again.

ACE

I went to a great Indian restaurant last night. The waiters were friendly to us and the walls were painted in a lovely shade of red. I had an onion bhaji to start with and it was really tasty. Then I had a delicious curry. After the meal the waiters brought us mints, which was good of them.

Eek!

SAME WORD TRAP

This is <u>loads better</u>. It's exactly the same piece of writing except it uses lots of <u>different</u> words instead of "nice" — so seems more <u>interesting</u>.

It's easy to fall into the trap of using the same word all the time — especially <u>adjectives</u> like "<u>nice</u>" or "<u>weird</u>". You've got to keep an eye out and make sure you don't do it.

Look Out For Verbs As Well As Adjectives

It's not just with the adjectives that you can choose from oodles of different words.

Look at this little piece of writing. It becomes a lot more interesting just by using two <u>new verbs</u> instead of repeating "ran" twice.

I ran to the post box with a letter, then I ran to the shop for some chocolate. After that I ran home so I wasn't late for tea.

I ran to the post box with a letter, then I hurried to the shop for some chocolate. After that I raced home so I wasn't late for tea.

Here's another example:

You could say **Jump**

or **Leap**   or **Bound**

Think up <u>different</u> words whenever you can — they make your writing <u>tons better</u>.

Use Different Words

Examiners get dead impressed by a few <u>fancy words</u>. If you can <u>use</u> some in your SAT, they'll think you're real clever. And that means <u>better marks</u>.

Clever Words Impress The Examiner

Using <u>different</u> words is a good start. If you can use <u>different</u> and <u>clever</u> words, you're laughing teacakes. Long and clever words can really improve your SAT marks.

United played *badly* on Saturday. → United played *lamentably* on Saturday.

The pitch was in a *poor* condition. → The pitch was in an *atrocious* condition.

The referee made some *very stupid* decisions. → The referee made some *exceedingly moronic* decisions.

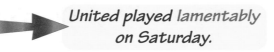

You can't use long fancy words <u>all</u> the time — that'd just sound <u>daft</u>. But you'll get extra marks if you throw them in <u>now and then</u>. So remember this rule:

sporadically *endeavour* *substitute* *concise*

Every now and then, try to replace a short and simple word with a long and clever one.

elementary *complex* *intellectual*

That is a more advantageous compilation of phraseology.

Of course, you have to know some <u>clever words</u> before you can use them in your SATs. Get into the habit of <u>looking up</u> words you don't know in the <u>dictionary</u>. Chances are, the more words you know, the better you'll do.

Don't Worry (Too Much) About Spelling Long Words

Generally speaking, spelling is <u>really important</u>, and if you don't spell well you <u>WILL</u> lose marks for it.

BUT: examiners like long words so much that even if you get the spelling slightly wrong, you'll still get <u>credit</u> for trying. If you want to use a long word but you're not sure you know how to spell it, then <u>don't shy away</u>. Give it a go.

And one last thing — <u>DON'T</u> use a long word if you're <u>not sure</u> what it means.

Johnny, what is the definition of infelicitous? / IN-FELL-ICARUS

Use long words? — OK, wooooorrdddsssss...

You'll get much better marks if you make your writing <u>interesting</u>. The first step is to use <u>different</u> words, then throw in some <u>long</u> and <u>clever</u> words and hey presto — it'll be fascinating.

Don't Be Boring

Here are a couple more tricks that'll help you make your writing more interesting.

Don't use "And" and "Then" Too Much

This is something loads of people do, but it makes your writing a great big <u>yawn</u>.

YAWN!

> *I went to the beach and I put on my trunks and I walked to the sea and the water was warm and I swam for an hour.*

Great trunks...

> Instead of using "and" all the time, try to use commas and full stops.

> *I went to the beach, put on my trunks and walked to the sea. The water was warm. I swam for an hour.*

> It's OK to use "and" and "then" sometimes — but not too much.

> *We went to the bank then we had a coffee and then we went back to the car. Then we drove to the supermarket and did some shopping, then we drove home.*

> After going to the bank, we had a coffee. *Then we went back to the car and drove to the supermarket. We did some shopping and drove home.*

> Changing the word order helps you not to use "then" all the time.

Don't Start All Your Sentences The Same Way

This is another thing that makes your writing <u>dull</u> and <u>boring</u>. You'll <u>lose marks</u> if you do it in the SAT.

> *There was a chill in the air as Jo walked towards the house. There was nobody around. There was a big oak door and Jo knocked on it. There was a scream from inside the house.*

> This says the same things, but in a more interesting way.

AAAHAHAHH

Mum's home early!

> *There was a chill in the air as Jo walked towards the house. Nobody was around. Jo knocked on the big oak door. A scream came from inside the house.*

Think of different ways to start your sentences. It isn't all that hard, and it makes your writing a whole lot more <u>interesting</u> to read.

Don't Be Boring

Interesting writing doesn't only use different words, it uses <u>sentences</u> of <u>different lengths</u>.

Use a *Variety* of *Short* and *Long* Sentences

Sometimes a <u>short</u> sentence works best and sometimes a <u>long</u> one does. <u>Neither</u> of them work well <u>all</u> of the time. It's best to use a <u>variety</u> of different lengths.

The important thing to <u>remember</u> is not to write all short sentences, and not to write all long sentences. They both make your writing <u>boring</u>.

WOOF   WOOF **W O O F**

These chunks of writing are as dull as dishwater. That's because the sentences are all short or all long.

All short: **DULL**

> *I was walking to the station. I needed to catch a train. It left at one o'clock. I checked my watch. I was late. I decided to run. The streets were busy. I kept having to dodge people. That slowed me down. I came to a busy road. I had to wait for the green crossing sign. It seemed to take ages. Finally I crossed the road. I got to the station. The train hadn't left. It was only five to one. I looked at my watch again. It was fast.*

All long: **DULL**

> *I was walking to the station because I needed to catch a train which left at one o'clock and I checked my watch and I was late so I decided to run but the streets were busy and I kept having to dodge people, which slowed me down. I came to a busy road where I had to wait for the green crossing sign and it seemed to take ages, but finally I crossed the road and got to the station where I saw the train hadn't left because it was only five to one so I looked at my watch again and it was fast.*

LOADS MORE INTERESTING   Some short, some long:

> *I was walking to the station. I needed to catch a train which left at one o'clock. I checked my watch and I was late so I decided to run, but the streets were busy and I kept having to dodge people, which slowed me down. I came to a busy road where I had to wait for the green crossing sign. It seemed to take ages. Finally I crossed the road and got to the station, where I saw the train hadn't left because it was only five to one. I looked at my watch again. It was fast.*

This is more like it. The mix of long and short sentences makes this version much more interesting to read.

Hmmm, looks a nice enough chap — a short sentence this time I think.

Make your writing more <u>interesting</u> — use sentences of different lengths.

Hunting wild pigs — nope, that'd be 'boaring'

These things make your writing <u>boring</u>: using "<u>and</u>" and "<u>then</u>" too much, <u>starting</u> your sentences the <u>same way</u>, and using <u>all long</u> sentences or <u>all short</u> sentences. Just don't do it.

Adjectives

Adjectives are great for making your writing more <u>interesting</u>. Whenever you get a question asking you to "<u>describe</u>" something, make sure you <u>cram</u> your answer with adjectives.

Describe Things with Adjectives

<u>Adjectives</u> are describing <u>words</u>. They're a quick and easy way to <u>spice up</u> your writing.

Just <u>one</u> little adjective can completely change the <u>impression</u> you get from a sentence.

I ate a meal.   I ate a *delicious* meal.   I ate a *disgusting* meal.

And with <u>three</u> or <u>four</u> adjectives, you can really start to build up a picture.

I ate a *delicious, sumptuous, lovingly-prepared* meal.

I ate a *disgusting, rancid, undercooked* meal.

Who needs to cook it?...

Adjectives give you a Picture

Have a look at this piece of writing. It's the <u>adjectives</u> that really tell you what this <u>place is like</u>. Without them you <u>wouldn't</u> get much of an idea at all.

Gone Fishing.

> Jordios is a *quiet*, *sleepy* village on the *remote* island of Toonos, forty miles from Athens. Miles of *unspoilt*, *sandy* beaches stretch along the *deserted* coastline. The air is thick with the *sweet* smell of pine trees, and you can sit in the shade of the *tall*, *elegant* cypress trees that grow all over the island.
> *Rickety* wooden fishing boats set off every morning from the *small*, *picturesque* harbour. The fishermen's faces are *gnarled* and *sunburnt*. In the evenings the locals gather in the *cosy*, *welcoming* tavernas for a *friendly* chat over a *refreshing* glass of ouzo, and a game of table top bungee jumping.

Jug Suppliers — they give you pitchers...

Adjectives are a great way of <u>describing</u> things effectively. If you get a question in your SAT that asks you to <u>describe</u> something, using plenty of <u>adjectives</u> is the key to getting good marks.

Comparing

You need more to describe things than just plain old adjectives.
Another good way to describe something is to compare it to something else.

Less Than, More Than, The Least, The Most...

Comparisons are a great way to build up a picture of something. They sound interesting and they create a big effect in your reader's mind. They're also loads of fun.

Lisa felt sick. Her face went green. → *Lisa felt sick. Her face went greener than an iceberg lettuce.*

It was very cold. → *It was colder than an Arctic winter.*

He was very bad at beach volleyball. → *He was the worst beach volleyball player I had ever seen.*

She was beautiful. → *She was the most beautiful woman this side of Stockport.*

The key to making a good comparison is to pick something sensible. It's no good saying "it was colder than a pair of scissors", or "Lisa's face went as green as a doorbell".

Careful — Don't Write "More Better"

There's one mistake that tons of people make but which will lose you loads of marks.

When you're making a comparison, you must EITHER say "more ... than" or "the most...", OR you use the form of the word that ends in "er" or "est". You DON'T do BOTH.

Ted is the cleverest boy in school.
NOT the "most cleverest".

You are the most sporty person I know.
NOT the "most sportiest".

I can't help thinking there's something different about that boy.

Suzanne is prettier than her sister.
NOT "more prettier".

You are more intelligent than a brick.
NOT "more intelligenter".

I am prettier than you.
Don't be daft Suzanne, you're green and your nose is enormous.

This rented house is the smallest — it's 'leased'...

Comparisons are another top way of making your writing more interesting — examiners love them. But don't get confused — you either use more/most, or you use the er/est ending. Not both.

More Comparing

You don't have to use "<u>more than</u>" or "<u>less than</u>" when you're making comparisons. Another way of doing it is to say one thing is <u>like</u> another. That can be really <u>effective</u> too.

Say that One Thing is Like Another

There are <u>two</u> ways of doing this.

(1) The first is to take an <u>adjective</u>, think of a <u>comparison</u>, and then instead of using "more" and "than", you use "<u>as</u>" and "<u>as</u>". You do it like this:

Anyone for Mud-Pool?

Beth felt as happy as a hippo in a mud pool.

That idea was as useless as a chocolate teapot.

Chocolate teapot — doesn't seem like such a bad idea to me.

(2) The other way of saying one thing is <u>like</u> another is nice and simple — you use the word "<u>like</u>".

Look, a chocolate teapot, ace.

Her eyes lit up like the sky on bonfire night.

I'd forgotten my gloves and soon my fingers were like blocks of ice.

It's Okay to Exaggerate to Make an Effect

Don't worry about <u>exaggerating</u> when you make a comparison. That's why it's so much <u>fun</u>.

Jack was as tall as a tree.

Freda was as old as the hills.

Trees are generally pretty tall, and hills are pretty old, so these are <u>good comparisons</u> to use. You don't <u>literally</u> mean that Jack was as tall as a tree or Freda was as old as a hill — but people will understand.

(If your comparisons had to be totally <u>accurate</u>, there'd be no point. You'd have to write stuff like "Jack was as tall as a six foot two inch tree", or "Freda was as old as a ninety-eight year old hill".)

I've told you a million times — stop exaggerating...

Remember the <u>two</u> ways to say that one thing is <u>similar</u> to another — use "<u>as ... as</u>" or use the word "<u>like</u>". It's OK to <u>exaggerate</u> when you make comparisons — that's what makes them <u>interesting</u>.

Speaking Figuratively

If you speak "literally", you mean exactly what you say. Saying something you don't literally mean is called speaking figuratively. We all do it — and it can really liven up your writing.

Say Things you don't Literally mean

When you speak figuratively, you talk about one thing as if it is something else.

This is another way of making a comparison. Instead of saying that one thing is like another thing, you talk about the first thing as if it actually is the other thing that you're comparing it to.

> Bob cried so hard that a river flowed down his cheeks.

> Sarah needed a glass of water — there was a desert in her mouth.

There wasn't literally a river flowing down Bob's cheeks, or a desert in Sarah's mouth.

This is a clever way of saying that Bob's tears were like a river, and Sarah's mouth was as dry as a desert.

Sometimes when you speak figuratively it seems to have nothing at all to do with what you actually mean — but it's obvious when you think about it.

> Dog Girl tried to delete the old files from her computer, but she wiped the entire hard drive by mistake. She had thrown the baby out with the bathwater.

Dog Girl hadn't actually gone near any real babies. This is just a figurative way of saying that in the process of throwing away something she didn't need, she got rid of something very important as well.

Don't Use Too Many Clichés — they Get Boring

Some figures of speech are used so often that they become boring.
They're called clichés.
You hear them a lot when people are talking about sport.

> I'm as sick as a parrot.

> The atmosphere's electric.

> It isn't over till the fat lady sings.

Well, I'm a fat electric singing parrot, that's NOT a cliché

You can get away with using some clichés in your SAT, but don't use too many — the examiner will think you haven't got anything original to say.

He said, "Speak figuratively," — I said, "5738492"...

Speaking figuratively means talking about one thing as if it's something else, and it's a great way to spice up your writing. Careful, though — don't use too many clichés. Be original if you can.

Revision Summary Questions

So now you know loads of tricks to help you make your writing interesting. It's important that you learn all this and remember to use it in the SAT writing questions. Imagine you're the examiner — if you've got to read something that's dull and boring, you're not going to give it many marks. But interesting writing isn't something you can do just like that — you have to practise it so it becomes natural. Make sure you can answer all these questions, and every time you write something, try to put what you've learned into action.

1) Is using the same word all the time: a) nice   b) nice   c) nice   d) incredibly boring?

2) Is the examiner going to be impressed by someone who can use clever words correctly?

3) Should you aim to use long and clever words:
   a) never   b) all the time   c) every now and then, but only when you know the meaning?

4) When you read a word and you don't know what it means, what should you do?

5) If you're in your SAT and you know a long and clever word that'd be really appropriate for something you're writing, but you're not 100% sure how to spell it, what should you do?

6) Which two words do you have to watch out for using too much?
   a) "and" and "then".
   b) "endogenous" and "exogenous".
   c) "Manchester" and "United".

7) Why is it a bad idea to start all your sentences the same way?

8) What do judges and SAT students have in common?
   a) they have to wear silly wigs.   b) they should try to use sentences of varying lengths.

9) Why are adjectives great?
   a) they make you a cup of tea in the morning.
   b) they help you to describe something.
   c) you can cuddle them and take them for walks and stuff.

10) Which of these comparisons works better?
   a) It was hotter than the Sahara Desert.   b) It was hotter than a piece of string.

11) Why?

12) Which of these comparisons works better?
   a) It was brighter than a candle.   b) It was brighter than a million suns.

13) Why?

14) Which of these is wrong?
   a) You're weirder than me.   b) She's my bestest friend.   c) He's more insane, though.
   d) I'm the most funniest.   e) We're the most charming.   f) They're much more better.

15) What are two ways of saying that one thing is similar to another?

16) Is it OK to exaggerate when you're making comparisons?

17) What's the difference between speaking figuratively and speaking literally?

18) When is it OK to use clichés?
   a) Now and again.
   b) Most of the time.
   c) Till the cows come home.

That's an interesting 'IT'...

Persuading

Sometimes you'll get a question in your SAT that asks you to write about <u>your opinions</u> — like in a <u>speech</u> or a <u>newspaper column</u>. That means you have to <u>write persuasively</u>.

Persuasive *Writing is Like* Selling *Something*

Persuasive writing is all about <u>making someone else agree</u> with your point of view. Trying to persuade someone to agree with you is exactly like trying to <u>sell</u> a product.

You need to sound <u>positive and certain</u> that you're right. If you're <u>half-hearted</u> and wishy-washy about what you're saying, no one is going to be <u>convinced</u>.

Make sure you've got enough good reasons to <u>back up your opinion</u>.

> You're not convincing anyone you half-hearted wimp.

> Well, just listen to you, you big chicken..!

You'll also need some <u>handy tricks</u> for presenting those opinions. <u>Here they are</u>.

Work Out the Opposite *View* — *Then Say It's* Wrong

A good way to start is to look at it from <u>the other point of view</u>. Think about why people might <u>not</u> agree with you — then you can work out how to <u>prove them wrong</u>.

Here's how you might plan a speech trying to <u>persuade</u> people to <u>support</u> a <u>ban</u> on foxhunting.

Notes: Reasons why people disagree with banning foxhunting
1. *Countryside jobs — but there aren't that many*
2. *Need to cull foxes — but there are more humane ways*
3. *Tradition — but so were bear-baiting and witch-burning*

These are reasons it should **NOT** be banned.

Here's how you can say these reasons are <u>wrong</u>.

And here's how you could write out one of those points.

<u>Why Foxhunting Should Be Banned</u>
Supporters of foxhunting say that it's a tradition. But in the past, it was traditional to burn witches and bait bears. Times change, and society moves on. Just because something is traditional is no reason to keep it.

Show that you've <u>thought</u> about what your opponents say and you still <u>disagree</u> with them. You'll have more chance of <u>persuading</u> other people that your <u>own</u> view is <u>right</u>.

Hit me with a wallet till I give in — 'purse'uasive...

Persuasive writing is all about <u>selling your point of view</u> to other people. A good way to start is to ask yourself what the <u>opposite arguments</u> are, write them down, and then say why they're <u>wrong</u>.

Exaggerating

When you're trying to <u>persuade</u> people to agree with you, it's a good idea to make your <u>own</u> points sound even <u>better</u> than they are, and your <u>opponents</u>' points seem <u>even worse</u>.

Exaggerate Your Good Points

It might sound a bit <u>unfair</u> to exaggerate how good your own arguments are. But <u>don't worry</u> — everyone does it. If you don't exaggerate, people will actually think your points are <u>weak</u>.

If you have a point worth making — do it with style.

This is a <u>great</u> point.

Version 1 — Rubbish:

Global warming could be <u>quite</u> a problem. <u>Some scientists</u> think the earth is getting warmer quite quickly. That <u>might mean</u> that <u>a fair bit</u> of farmland turns into desert, so <u>people</u> might <u>not have enough food</u>.

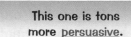

This one is tons more <u>persuasive</u>.

It uses <u>strong</u> words like as "<u>massive</u>", "<u>frightening</u>" and "<u>huge</u>" instead of <u>weak</u> ones like "<u>quite</u>" or "<u>a fair bit</u>".

It says "<u>many</u> scientists" instead of "some".

It says "<u>will</u>" and "<u>huge areas</u>" instead of "might" and "a fair bit"

It talks about "<u>billions</u> of people" instead of just saying "people".

It uses the <u>scary</u> word "<u>starve</u>" instead of "not have enough food".

Version 2 — Good:

Global warming is a <u>massive</u> threat to the very future of humanity. <u>Many scientists</u> believe the earth is getting warmer at a <u>frightening</u> rate. If this continues, <u>huge</u> areas of farmland <u>will</u> turn into desert, causing <u>billions of people</u> to <u>starve</u>.

Be careful, though — you're allowed to exaggerate, but you're <u>not</u> allowed to <u>lie</u>. You <u>can't</u> say things that <u>aren't true</u>, like "global warming will cause aliens to take over the Earth".

If you say things that <u>obviously aren't true</u>, people won't trust the rest of your arguments.

Make Your Opponents Sound Crazy

Putting your opponents' point of view in your own words is a good way of making them sound bad.

You can also <u>exaggerate</u> what people who disagree say, to make them sound <u>crazy</u>.

Some businessmen believe we have no responsibility to the environment. They think it doesn't matter if we keep on churning out deadly greenhouse gases. All they care about is making profits.

You can be <u>harsh</u> — as long as you don't <u>tell any actual lies</u>.

10 out of 10 for exagge — a high exagge-rating...

Exaggeration is a <u>crucial trick</u> for good persuasive writing. You can use it to make <u>yourself</u> sound <u>good</u>, and make your <u>opponents</u> sound <u>bad</u>. But make sure you <u>don't lie</u>. That's all there is to it.

Persuasive Tricks

Here are <u>three nifty tricks</u> which will make your persuasive writing a whole load better.

Talk About "We" and "Us" Whenever You Can

Surely we all agree that what's best for us is to give me the cake?

If you want someone to agree with you, it's a <u>good idea</u> to make them think they have <u>a lot in common</u> with you.

Using the words "<u>we</u>" and "<u>us</u>" is a sneaky way to make your audience feel like they <u>ought to be on your side</u>.

Surely <u>we</u> all agree that cruelty to animals is wrong.

These are much better than "<u>I think</u> that cruelty..." or "...that affects <u>some people</u>" would be.

Pollution is an issue that affects all of <u>us</u>.

Use Questions To Make Your Points

<u>Asking</u> people something is a <u>great</u> way to make them sit up and take notice — even though you don't want an answer.

The trick is to <u>say the question</u> so that there can <u>only</u> be <u>one possible answer</u>.

Does anyone really want to live in a world without clean air to breathe?

No one in their right minds would say "yes" to this.

Alternatively, you can <u>ask a question</u> then go on to <u>answer it yourself</u>.

And why doesn't the government do anything about it? I'll tell you why. It's because they want big businesses to give them donations.

Use "Magic Threes" — Three Adjectives

<u>Three</u> is a <u>magic number</u> when you're writing <u>persuasively</u>. If you use three <u>adjectives</u> to describe something, it sounds much <u>more effective</u> than only using one or two.

THREE

Fossil fuels are dirty, dangerous and outdated.

Renewable energy is clean, safe and efficient.

Lorries that make you agree — persuasive trucks...

Talk about "<u>we</u>" and "<u>us</u>", use <u>questions</u> to make your points, and use adjectives in <u>groups of three</u>. These are great tricks — listen to politicians' speeches and you'll hear them all the time.

Don't Be Rude

Even if you're <u>really convinced</u> about something, you're not going to <u>persuade</u> anyone by being <u>rude</u>. People will <u>only</u> want to listen to what you say if you're <u>polite</u>.

Keep Your Writing Polite

If they don't agree with you, being <u>rude</u> to them isn't going to help. It'll just get their backs up.

Recycling is very important. Anybody who doesn't recycle their waste is stupid and selfish.

NO! People will be put off and stop listening.

Much better. People will listen and you might change their minds.

Recycling is very important. It's something every one of us can do to help our planet.

No matter how strongly you feel about something, <u>always</u> be <u>polite</u>.

Keep Criticisms General And Impersonal

Don't make <u>direct attacks</u> on your <u>opponents</u>. It'll make you sound angry and <u>aggressive</u>, and anyone who's <u>neutral</u> will be <u>turned off by your attitude</u>. And that includes the examiner.

If you think monkey juggling is acceptable, I think you're wrong.

Instead of this, say this...

Some people think monkey juggling is acceptable, but I think they're wrong.

...or better still, this.

It is sometimes said that monkey juggling is acceptable, but I think that's wrong.

Who's juggling WHAT?

Make Your Positive Points Personal

...But for <u>positive points</u>, be <u>as personal as you like</u>. Using "<u>you</u>" gets your audience to sit up and listen, and using "<u>we</u>" makes them think they're <u>on your side</u>.

You can make a difference by not buying this company's products. Together we can bring this awful practice to an end.

This sort of <u>personal</u> language is especially <u>effective</u> when you use it as an ending.

Don't make a rude-imentary mistake...

Always remember to <u>be polite</u> in your persuasive writing, and make your <u>negative</u> points <u>impersonal</u>. Being <u>rude and aggressive</u> rubs people up the <u>wrong way</u> — and it'll lose you marks.

SECTION TEN — PERSUASIVE WRITING

Revision Summary Questions

This is the last section about the writing section of your SAT, and the last section of the whole book (Woo Hoo!) — just think if you've learned everything in the book so far, you'll have learned all the skills you need to get through the SAT. But before you can say that, you have to make sure you know this section properly. It's well worth it because chances are you'll get a question in the SAT that wants you to write persuasively — whether it's a speech, a magazine article or a letter. And persuasive writing is something you can get really good at just by learning the tricks in these pages.

1) What should you do after you have listed the reasons why people might disagree with you?

2) How can you make your opponents' beliefs sound crazy?

3) Which of these is a good use of exaggeration?
   a) "The arms industry causes some suffering in the world".
   b) "The arms industry is directly responsible for causing untold misery to millions".
   c) "The arms industry likes to kidnap newborn babies and roast them on a spit".
   What is wrong with the other two sentences?

4) If I said it was a good idea to tell lies about your opponents, would I be right?

5) Why is it a good idea to use "we" and "us" a lot in persuasive writing?

6) Which of these would be a good question to use in a piece of persuasive writing?
   a) "What is the capital of Estonia?"
   b) "Would you like your children to grow up in a world without wild flowers?"
   c) "Can anyone lend me a fiver?"

7) What makes it such an effective question?

8) What's the other good trick to use with questions?

9) Is the idea of using three adjectives to describe something:
   a) daft.
   b) pointless and strange.
   c) clever, valuable and effective?

10) What would you write to try to convince someone who thinks that you should be rude in persuasive writing that it's better to be polite?
   a) "Don't be idiotic, you pea-brained fool, that idea stinks."
   b) "Many people find that being polite works much better."

11) Why is it a good idea to keep your criticisms general and impersonal?

12) Can your positive points be personal?

13) What is an especially effective time to use personal language?
   a) As an ending.
   b) Eight o'clock, but ten o'clock on Thursdays and Fridays.
   c) When asking to borrow a fiver.

So, what's so great about purse-wading again?

Index

Index

P

paragraphs 32, 35, 66
personal 89
persuade 11, 87, 89
persuading 86
persuasive tricks 88
persuasive writing 86
Pharaohs 1
picture 10, 81
pictures with words 81
plan 61, 62
plan your essay 34
poetry 44
polite 89
poodles 18
positive points 89
preparing your answer 34
prose 44
punctuation 43, 70, 75

Q

quote 28
question 8
question marks 70, 75
quoting 1, 24, 26, 29, 34, 35,
    52, 53, 54, 74

R

rat on a stick 68
reading 1
reasons 12, 26
relationships
    between characters 47
rhymed verse 45
rhythm 45
riddles 46
rude 89

S

scenes 36, 53
scream 78
see it, say it 22
sentences 35, 71, 72
set scenes 33
Shakespeare 32-57
Shakespeare — huge
    revision question 55
Shakespeare question 33
Shakespeare's language 41 - 46
shiny new point 66
short and long sentences 80
short comprehension
    questions 4, 19, 20
short quotes 30
short sentences 79
short writing questions 60
show the audience
    what's going on 51
shut up 72
simple points 1, 2
simple words 77
skateboards for dogs 17
snow doughnuts 25
sound — plays 51
soy sauce 73
speaking lines 51, 52
speaking — how characters talk 48
speech 74
speech marks 27, 28, 74, 75
spellings 35, 78
stage directions 38
starting your sentences 79
state the obvious 2, 24
steak and chips 69
strong words 87
style 4, 11, 63
style questions 4, 20
suspense 8
sympathy 15

T

talking — how characters speak 48
teacakes 78
termites 11
theme questions 53, 54
then 79
things characters do 47
three adjectives 88
three golden rules 1
toilet 28
tragedies 36
tricks of persuasive language 49

U

understand 3, 19
understanding language —
    shakespeare 51
underwater snooker 11
use your own words 27

V

verbs 71, 77

W

ways that characters speak 48
"we" and "us" 88
weird 77
we're 73
what characters say about
    each other 47
who the characters are 48
whole question 58
why characters do things 47
wild pigs 80
wobblies 41
woof 80
word for word 28
word order 79
writing letters 64
writing questions 58
writing styles 63